VEGAN MEDITERRANEAN COOKBOOK

ZUCCHINI BOATS WITH COUSCOUS STUFFING, P. 115

VEGAN MEDITERRANEAN

COOKBOOK

Essential Vegiterranean Recipes
for the Ultimate Healthy Lifestyle

TESS CHALLIS

FOREWORD BY VICTORIA MORAN
PHOTOGRAPHY BY BECKY STAYNER

ROCKRIDGE
PRESS

Interior and Cover Designer: Peatra Jariya
Art Producer: Karen Beard
Editor: Rachel Feldman
Production Manager: Riley Hoffman
Production Editor: Melissa Edeburn

Photography © 2019 Becky Stayner. Food styling by Kathleen Phillips. Author photo courtesy of Melissa Schwartz.

ISBN: Print 978-1-64152-614-2 | eBook 978-1-64152-615-9

This book is dedicated to you and to everyone who wants to live a healthier, more joyous life—and to do so while eating some of the most delicious foods on the planet!

AVOCADO-CITRUS SALAD, P. 81

ROASTED PINE NUT ORZO, P. 109

CONTENTS

FOREWORD

It's easy to look at the array of vegan cookbooks and restaurant offerings available today and see two apparently contradictory options:

1. *The anything-goes-if-no-animal-was-harmed point of view.* This option is epicurean veganism. Foods that are highly processed, deep-fried, and super sweet get a green light, alongside healthier fare. People who choose this equal-opportunity eating style lessen animal suffering, protect the planet, and free their bodies from the burden of exogenous cholesterol, found only in animal foods, and from animal protein, shown through the work of T. Colin Campbell and other researchers to turn on cancer genes.

2. *The whole-foods-plant-based-no-oil strategy* (sometimes expanded to SOS: no sugar, oil, or salt). This is the dietary choice of those for whom preventing or reversing heart disease or other maladies is top priority. Extensive scientific data shows that this way of eating, focused on fresh fruits, vegetables, whole grains, and legumes, simply prepared, can reverse coronary artery disease, something once believed impossible. Folks who stick with this dietary regimen, even though others may regard it as austere, often have breathtaking turnarounds of disease and exceptional well-being into advanced age.

These options put someone like me in a bit of a quandary. I am a vegan for the animals and, accordingly, I applaud every beef-like burger, sharp and savory nut-based cheese, and tempting vegan pastry that exists. These foods are making the world kinder. Even so, I rarely eat them. My family has a long history of heart disease, coupled with diabetes. I need to be careful. And yet, asceticism is not my jam. In my thirties, I overcame a long-standing binge-eating disorder by replacing the need to use food as a fix with love for myself and others. I began eating in a spirit of celebration, rather than deprivation.

The vegan Mediterranean approach, as described and brought deliciously to life here by Tess Challis, is poised to be the Next Big Thing. The traditional Mediterranean diet has reams of scientific support for promoting health. The veganized version has not yet been well studied, but it eliminates animal protein and cholesterol, slashes saturated fat from which the body makes cholesterol, and is likely to be lower in overall fat than its lauded predecessor. In addition, it includes even more fruits, vegetables, and beans, with their wealth of vitamins, minerals, fiber, and antioxidants. Could it be that a good thing just got a whole lot better?

In addition, as Challis explains clearly and then illustrates with her delectable recipes, this food is satisfying for body and soul. Dishes in the culinary heritage of Greece, Italy, and the Middle East have flavor and texture profiles that leave nothing out. This is comfort food at its best: enticing, filling, nourishing, complete.

Perhaps you want to use this cookbook as a source of easy and compliment-catching recipes to supplement the way you eat and feed your family now. Or maybe you're looking to it as a springboard for going vegan Mediterranean all the time. Either way, you can expect your meals to reflect some of the color and beauty and joy of this idyllic part of the world, and you can expect your life to be a bit more *bellissimo,* too.

Victoria Moran
CHHC, AADP, author of *Main Street Vegan* and *The Love-Powered Diet,* host of the Main Street Vegan podcast, and director of Main Street Vegan Academy

INTRODUCTION

Although I've been vegan since 1991, I haven't always been a healthy one—in fact, I was an *obese* vegan for most of my twenties. Yes, that's an actual thing! Onion rings, French fries, potato chips, chocolate cake, and other highly processed foods—combined with a lack of exercise—didn't exactly do my body good. Looking back, I noticed that my poor and excessive eating coincided with the times I ate the least whole, natural foods.

Yes, I was still eating a vegan diet, which I believed in then as much as I do now. Avoiding animal products is one of the most powerful things we can do to prolong our lifespan, preserve the environment, and save animals from unnecessary suffering. Yet, despite feeling good about those aspects of veganism, I was pretty unhappy about the unhealthiness of my approach to eating. I remember thinking, "There has to be a way to be a healthy, fit vegan but also still enjoy food." And yes, spoiler alert—this is where the Mediterranean lifestyle came in to work its magic.

What comes to mind when you think of the Mediterranean? For me, it's gorgeous blue sky and ocean, next to white shores and countryside. I also think of bright foods that are rich in flavor but high in nutrients (I'm talking to you, baba ghanoush and tabbouleh). I think of fresh air, sunshine, exercise, and joyful people. The vibrancy of life in the Mediterranean region isn't a coincidence; it has everything to do with the region's natural landscape, which is responsible for the beautiful climate as well as the beautiful produce. That produce is the reason that the Mediterranean diet has historically been, and remains, the best plant-based diet in the world. A Mediterranean diet, with its bold flavors and rewarding lifestyle, perfectly exemplifies how enjoyable (and supremely healthy) a vegan diet can be.

So, a Mediterranean lifestyle was essentially what saved me. I'd always been a foodie, but I hadn't embraced a diet that allowed me to eat truly delicious foods while staying nutritionally balanced. When I began eating less processed food and more fresh food (particularly organic vegetables and legumes), I regained my health, lost weight, and was able to finally love food that loved me back. To this day, I'm so grateful for this way of eating. I'm a huge believer that we absolutely must *enjoy* the foods in our healthy diet, or we simply won't be able to stick with it long term.

When we give ourselves full permission to truly enjoy food—and nourish ourselves with exercise and nutrient-dense, fresh, plant-based foods—our bodies thrive. We gain energy, strengthen our immune system, and give ourselves the best chance to prevent disease and illness. My goal in this book is to inspire you to embrace a joyful, healthy way of life, no matter where you are currently on your food and health journey. Making the choice to adopt a Mediterranean-inspired lifestyle will reward you with happiness and excellent health for years to come.

1

THE VEGAN MEDITERRANEAN WAY

In this chapter, we'll take off our shoes, grab some tea, and get comfy with the principles of a plant-based Mediterranean diet. Have no fear! We'll dive into the basics, and by the time you're done reading this chapter, you'll understand what the Mediterranean lifestyle is all about as well as how easy and enjoyable eating a healthy, vegan, Mediterranean diet can be.

Because your health is affected by more than just the foods you eat, we'll also cover the nonfood basics of a holistically healthy Mediterranean lifestyle, which include exercise, community, and a calm attitude. We'll also demystify the foods that make up a Mediterranean diet, so you can feel confident and comfortable whipping up masterpieces in your own kitchen. Are you ready to start the next chapter of your life? Let's begin!

THE VEGAN MEDITERRANEAN DIET

It's becoming increasingly evident in our modern world that a diet rich in meat and dairy products isn't sustainable. Consuming animal products has been linked to a decrease in lifespan expectancy, increased cancer risk, unnecessary (and, unfortunately, excessive) animal suffering, and environmental destruction.

In a comprehensive study, Oxford University scientist Joseph Poore (who led the study) stated, "A vegan diet is probably the single biggest way to reduce your impact on planet earth; not just greenhouse gases, but global acidification, eutrophication, land use, and water use. It is far bigger than cutting down on your flights or buying an electric car."

Veganism even helps combat world hunger. It's estimated that 700 million tons of food that could be consumed by humans goes to livestock each year. Many studies suggest that if our world went vegan, the epidemic of human hunger would be eradicated. A vegan diet also helps conserve water (it takes up to 200 times more water to produce a pound of beef than it does to produce plant-based foods). Quinoa, anyone?

And, of course, a plant-based diet isn't just good for the planet, it's good for our bodies. Vegan diets can reduce the risk of type 2 diabetes—and even reverse diabetes in many cases. Veganism is also associated with a lower rate of heart disease and cancer risk. And the high levels of antioxidants (and low levels of inflammatory foods) in a whole-food vegan diet can do wonders to reduce inflammation in general, as well as the pain of arthritis.

This is why it's no surprise that more and more people are turning toward a vegan diet. In fact, it's happening in record numbers. As an old-school vegan (one who's been eschewing animal products for nearly three decades), I never thought I'd see the day when restaurant chains would be promoting vegan options and celebrities would be endorsing plant-based eating—and even more medical professionals would be recommending the nutritional and environmental superiority of a vegan diet.

However, it's absolutely possible to be an unhealthy vegan—as I was for most of my twenties. There are so many unhealthy processed foods available today, and if you eat them in excess, you won't be able to enjoy the full (and fabulous) benefits of a healthy vegan diet. But I'm no purist, either: If you try to eat too perfectly, you may end up feeling bored and restricted. A vegan Mediterranean diet is truly a wonderfully balanced way to achieve the best of all worlds—health *and* deliciousness, as well as a lower environmental impact.

And rest assured, if you're new to all of this and feeling overwhelmed, please know that it's okay to begin the process without expecting perfection overnight. In fact, it took me a few months to completely stick with vegan eating after I initially made the effort. I had plenty of stumbles before it finally stuck. But doing it at my own pace and discovering more and more delicious foods along the way led me to a way of eating and living that became much easier (and more delicious) over time. So, be kind to yourself and know that, yes, you absolutely can do this! And you'll be so darn glad you did.

Vegiterranean Origins

Here's a bit of history you may not know: The origins of the word *vegan* actually go back further than the defined concept of a Mediterranean diet. Donald Watson, founder of the Vegan Society, coined the word in 1944. He took the first and last letters of the word "vegetarian" to create this new version of vegetarianism. The American scientist Dr. Ancel Keys started explaining the benefits of the Mediterranean diet in the 1950s, but it didn't become popular in the United States until the 1990s. The concept of a Mediterranean diet was developed to reflect food patterns that were typical of Crete, most of Greece, and southern Italy in the early 1960s.

Surprisingly, the specific origins of the Mediterranean diet are somewhat lost in time because they blur into the eating habits of the Middle Ages, where the ancient Roman tradition—on the model of the Greek—relied on bread, wine, oil, vegetables, and a preference for fish over meat.

The Mediterranean diet has always lent itself well to plant-based eating, but it's only recently that combining a vegan and Mediterranean diet has become "a thing." Julieanna Hever, also known as the Plant-Based Dietician (and unofficially known as a plant-based goddess!), coined the term *Vegiterranean* with her 2014 book *The Vegiterranean Diet,* the first resource to really define and explore how powerful this diet combination is. It's a brilliant educational resource for those looking for in-depth nutritional information. As vegan eating continues to gain in popularity, and the Mediterranean diet remains as popular as ever, it makes sense that a combination of the two is finally getting attention from nutritionists, bloggers, and household cooks alike.

BENEFITS OF THE ULTIMATE HEALTHY LIFESTYLE

These are just five of the seemingly infinite number of benefits to the Mediterranean lifestyle:

1. **More energy.** If you're eating a plant-based diet rich in fresh, Mediterranean whole foods, you will be far less likely to experience that afternoon energy slump, often caused by processed foods high in refined sugars.

2. **Lower cholesterol overall.** Your overall cholesterol will likely go down more quickly than you'd expect (and your good, or HDL, cholesterol will often increase).

3. **Glowing skin.** Avoiding inflammatory foods in favor of eating lots of vibrant plant-based whole foods (including plenty of fruits and veggies) will do wonders for your skin. Vitamins A, C, and E are especially rejuvenating!

4. **Stronger immunity.** You'll be less susceptible to colds and other nuisances—a vegan Mediterranean diet is packed with immune-boosting vitamins and minerals, and thus great for the immune system.

5. **Healthy weight maintenance.** You'll be more likely to maintain a healthy weight with ease. Alkalinizing foods such as lemon, vegetables, and beans naturally help us keep excess weight off, and the absence of processed foods can help us stay fit for a lifetime.

A BREATH OF MEDITERRANEAN AIR

The Mediterranean diet is one of the most studied diets of all time and is ranked among the healthiest. Because of its emphasis on plant-based foods such as fruits, nuts, vegetables, legumes, seeds, and lemons, most experts agree that this way of eating reigns supreme. As opposed to fads and trends that come and go, the Mediterranean diet is a solid, scientifically backed way of eating that has stood the test of time. This is due in no small part to the fact that it's actually an enjoyable diet. With its use of vibrant flavors and healthy fats, the Mediterranean diet is able to highlight plant-based foods better than any other diet. So, much like the refreshing breeze of the Mediterranean air, the flavors of the Mediterranean can refresh a vegan diet. Breathe it in and know that you're choosing a time-tested (and thoroughly enjoyable!) way of eating.

The Traditional Mediterranean Diet

What's generally meant by a Mediterranean diet is one that's heavily plant based (high in fruits, nuts, legumes, vegetables, and whole grains). A *traditional* Mediterranean diet also includes fish and poultry at least twice a week, and red meat no more than a few times each month. It recommends replacing butter (and other cholesterol-rich fats) with olive oil. The focus here isn't on limiting total fat consumption, but instead on making wise choices about the types of fat consumed. The Mediterranean diet discourages saturated fats and hydrogenated oils (trans fats), because both are strongly implicated in cases of heart disease.

In a traditional Mediterranean diet, you'll also find moderate inclusion of red wine, but low overall intakes of eggs and sweets. Dairy products are typically allowed, but also in moderate amounts. Essentially, it's a way of eating that encourages balanced eating, lots of healthy fats and plant-based foods, and an overall enjoyment of life.

That Mediterranean philosophy of overall enjoyment goes beyond just the diet itself, extending to general principles for healthy living. This is why the diet is often thought of as a whole lifestyle, which promotes daily activity, social eating, and mindfulness. We'll get into the specifics of the lifestyle later in this chapter.

Vegan Eats, Mediterranean Style

Let's get to the (vegan) meat of the matter now: What makes those traditional Mediterranean guidelines so healthy, and how do the best of them apply to a vegan diet?

First of all, we have the obvious common denominator: the heavy reliance on plant-based foods. In both a traditional Mediterranean diet and a vegan diet, superstars like vegetables, fruits, nuts, seeds, legumes, and whole grains take the main stage. This is optimal, because these foods are all high in fiber, cholesterol free, and nutrient dense. They're also antioxidant rich and more likely to help you curb your hunger on fewer calories (because they're so nutritious and full of fiber).

Both diets also ask that meat, eggs, and dairy products be limited, although veganism, of course, eschews them completely. Anytime you eliminate (or even reduce) animal products, you slash your risk for disease and health problems. *How great is that?* And both a Mediterranean diet and veganism opt for zero-cholesterol oils (especially olive) rather than animal-based fats. As you can probably guess, this is good news because your cholesterol profile will thank you for it.

And, of course, in both diets, it's wise to move your body (yes, exercise) and limit your consumption of alcohol. The more active you are, the higher your metabolism will be, and the more you'll be able to enjoy a vibrant, strong physique. Plus, the fun principle (one that I really adore) of exercise in the Mediterranean philosophy is that you should enjoy it. Don't just exercise because you have to (or worse, because you dislike your body). Instead, exercise because you *get* to, and because you *love* your body.

THE HEALTHIEST PLACE ON EARTH

In his book *The Blue Zones: Lessons for Living Longer from the People Who've Lived the Longest,* Dan Buettner identified five regions where people tend to live much longer than average. And, I'm sure you saw this coming—two of these blue zones are in the Mediterranean: Icaria, Greece, and Sardinia, Italy. The other three are Okinawa, Japan; Loma Linda, California; and the Nicoya Peninsula, Costa Rica. These extraordinarily healthy places produce a relatively high rate of centenarians (people who live to 100 years old or more), and their residents also suffer a fraction of the diseases that are common in most other parts of the world, thus enjoying better health for a longer period of time.

The people inhabiting these blue zones share common lifestyle characteristics that contribute to their longevity and well-being. Some include:

- a primarily plant-based diet (that invariably includes legumes)

- less cigarette smoking

- regular physical activity

- moderate caloric intake

- minimal amounts of alcohol, including wine

- a happy social life (and a sense of purpose)

- stress reduction

It's no coincidence, then, that a vegan Mediterranean diet (and lifestyle) gives you the best chance for a long, happy life!

Meat alternatives like tofu or tempeh instead of meat

No eggs—flax eggs sometimes used as a substitute

No cheese made from animal milk

Milk alternatives like coconut milk, nut milks, oat milk, flax milk, or soy milk

Desserts don't always minimize saturated fat and refined sugar

No honey. Sweeteners can include granulated sugar, agave nectar, coconut sugar, or maple syrup

Some vegan foods are processed

No butter

Nuts and seeds

Plant-based sweeteners like pomegranates or dates

Healthy oils like olive oil and grapeseed oil, rather than saturated fats

Pulses like beans and legumes

Fresh vegetables of all kinds, including eggplant, tomatoes, potatoes, and leafy greens

Whole grains like farro, barley, bulgur, and wheat berries

Balsamic, red and white wine, and cider vinegars

Pasta and forms of bread, such as pita, flatbreads, and loaves

Herbs and spices to give dishes bold flavor

Butter sometimes used

Wine, in moderation, although not all wine is vegan

Fresh and dried fruits

Eggs

Honey commonly used in both sweet and savory dishes

Yogurt and milk from animals

Unprocessed and minimally processed foods

Animal proteins like shellfish, fish, protein, and, in moderation, lean red meat

A variety of cheeses, eaten in moderation—mostly sheep's and goat's milk cheeses, like feta and halloumi, as well as more traditional cow's milk cheeses like ricotta, Parmesan, and mozzarella

Desserts that emphasize fresh fruit and minimize saturated fat and refined sugar

MEDITERRANEAN

FOODS TO EMBRACE

Now that you're starting to feel excited about the benefits of a vegan Mediterranean life-style, it's time to think about the best foods to incorporate into your diet. And if this brings up the thought: "Uh oh, what do I have to give up?" I want to assure you that my approach isn't one of deprivation, but of abundance.

A big turning point for me in adopting a health-promoting vegan Mediterranean diet was when I realized that what I *focused* on was of utmost importance. For example, I'd been fixated on saying goodbye to my beloved Olive Garden cheese sticks. But when I realized that, in truth, I was actually enjoying my new plant-based foods even more, I decided to shift what I was putting my attention on. I decided to keep the ideal foods in the forefront of my mind, embracing and emphasizing those, rather than thinking about the old foods.

Here are a few reasons I love this approach:

- You naturally crowd out unhealthy foods when you're focused on vibrant, fresh foods. You automatically eat less of the not-so-great stuff when you begin to fill your plate with the good stuff more and more often.

- The healthier you eat, the more your taste buds will adjust. The old, unhealthy foods stop tasting good, and the new foods begin to be what you crave instead.

- And speaking of cravings, when you eat lots of fresh fruits, vegetables, legumes, and other plant-based foods, you'll automatically begin to lose your cravings for less healthy foods. Your body will start asking for the good stuff and preferring it.

A vegan Mediterranean diet brings out the best of plant-based eating, with beautiful fruits and vegetables at the forefront. Here are a few staples of this way of eating:

Chickpeas and other legumes: Chickpeas are absolutely amazing! Their versatility is unpar-alleled, as they can be added to smoothies, made into luscious chocolate desserts, roasted as a snack, made into an entrée or salad, or puréed to create a luscious hummus. They're chock-full of fiber, which fills you up and helps regulate blood sugar. Other beans common in Mediterranean cooking include lentils, fava beans, lima beans, and white beans. I can't say enough good things about legumes—they're the perfect food to put at the forefront of a satisfying, delicious diet that will also help you stay trim and energized.

Lemons: These little rays of sunshine create such a pop of flavor in so many dishes. I basically can't live without lemons, so please don't make me. And as such, I hope you'll forgive (and hopefully love) the liberal use of lemons in this book—there's just nothing like them to add a bright, scrumptious flavor to a wide variety of recipes, both sweet and savory. Plus, lemons are not only high in vitamin C, but also alkalinizing, detoxifying, and immune boosting. Be sure to use fresh lemon juice instead of bottled, as it makes all the difference in flavor and nutrition.

Fresh herbs: Rosemary, basil, dill, mint, and oregano are a few of my favorite herbs, but there are many others as well. The wonderful thing about fresh herbs is that they add loads of flavor to so many dishes but have zero negatives. They're just pure, chlorophyll-rich, antioxidant-filled goodness. I like to use them in sweet as well as savory dishes. I recommend adding them to dishes at the last minute instead of cooking them for long periods, so as not to dim their bright flavors.

Nuts and seeds: These healthy-fat staples add so much richness and depth to dishes. They're excellent sources of omega-3s and other nutrients, and as with all plant-based foods, contain zero cholesterol. You can eat them whole or blend them into all sorts of things. Sesame seeds are what make up tahini, and cashews are great roasted as a snack, or raw as a neutral-flavored base for savory creams, vegan cheeses, cheesecakes, and sweet sauces. You'll also find pistachios, macadamias, and other nuts in this book.

Garlic: Oh, garlic. Why are you so good to me? Garlic is just the thing to take any savory dish to the next level of flavor, plus it's absolutely packed with goodness. It helps detoxify the body, works as an immune booster, and lowers cholesterol. It has antioxidant properties and also helps regulate blood pressure and blood sugar levels. Use garlic in dips, dressings, entrées, sides, and snacks—basically in just about anything but chocolate. Please, not in chocolate.

Olives: Yummy, yummy olives can really round out a dish. Be sure to use a high-quality olive such as Kalamata, because it makes all the difference. A good olive will please your palate with a divine flavor and just the right amount of salt, whereas a canned black olive will taste "tinny" and lack depth of flavor. Use olives to garnish salads, creamy dips, and Greek plates or eat them plain with a crusty slice of bread and some olive oil.

Tomatoes: We see a lot of tomatoes in Greek cuisine, and they pair so beautifully with fresh herbs, garlic, legumes, and vegetables. Tomatoes are especially wonderful when in season, and contain the antioxidant lycopene, which reduces the risk of heart disease and cancer. They're also high in vitamin C, potassium, and folate.

Leafy green vegetables: These powerhouses of nutrition are an essential part of a healthy vegan Mediterranean diet. You'll see lots of kale and spinach in this book, but I encourage you to experiment with the vast variety of greens and find your favorites. They're all great sources of iron, chlorophyll, beta-carotene, and other important nutrients.

Whole grains: A Mediterranean diet includes healthy whole grains, as they're an important part of a balanced plate. Grains often get a bad rap, but I believe that's because people confuse refined grains with whole grains—and there's a big difference. Whole grains (such as brown rice, quinoa, and wheat) are higher in fiber, vitamins, and overall nutrients as compared to refined grains (such as white rice and white bread).

NUTRITIONAL CONSIDERATIONS

When I first went vegan, I was worried about getting enough nutrients, but then I began to really read up on the subject. What I discovered greatly eased my mind: If we're eating a plant-based diet composed mostly of whole foods (and are getting enough calories), it's very easy to meet all of our nutritional needs. In fact, every time I've had my levels tested over the decades, they've always been high. And what do I supplement with? Just organic vegetables, fruits, and whole plant foods. Nature has our back!

Of course, everyone is different, so if you're not comfortable with my no-supplements approach, it won't hurt to use them. Opt for natural brands that incorporate whole plants (such as spirulina and other superfoods) whenever possible.

Here are some commonly asked questions related to nutrition on a vegan diet:

HOW DO I GET OMEGA-3S WITHOUT FISH?

Omega-3 fatty acids are also found in flax, walnuts, algae, and hemp, among other items. And bonus—plant-based sources of omega-3s are also considered much safer. Even the most prominent physicians have questioned the safety of salmon and other fish; Dr. Oz suggests that we turn to the source (algae, which is what salmon themselves eat) to avoid overfishing and mercury.

HOW WILL I GET ENOUGH CALCIUM WITHOUT COW'S MILK? WHAT ABOUT OSTEOPOROSIS?

Interestingly, societies with the highest rates of osteoporosis are those that consume the most animal products. In societies that consume little or no dairy products, this disease (wrongly linked to inadequate calcium intake) is practically unheard of. Osteoporosis primarily results from the intake of too much animal protein, robbing the body of calcium. In other words, the less animal protein we consume, the less calcium we need. Plus, many plant foods contain calcium, including sesame, tofu, and kale and other greens.

A BALANCED VEGAN MEDITERRANEAN PLATE

I often get asked what a healthy plate should look like. It can be surprisingly confusing. In the spirit of demystifying that, I present the following guidelines for you. However, keep in mind that nutritional balance isn't just about one meal. It's okay to have unconventional meals here and there (such as a big salad for breakfast or a variety of dips for dinner) as long as your overall day ends up resembling a balanced plate.

Veggies on ½ of your plate. Make *at least* half of your plate nonstarchy vegetables and include lots of leafy greens. Also, think "rainbow!" (Try to vary your vegetables so you're eating a rainbow of colors whenever possible.)

Proteins on ¼ of your plate. A quarter of your plate should be plant-based proteins, especially legumes and beans. They'll fill you up without making you feel stuffed!

Healthy fats on ⅛ of your plate. Up to an eighth of your plate can include healthy fats (primarily whole foods such as nuts and seeds, but healthier oils such as olive are fine, too).

Whole grains on ⅛ of your plate. The final eighth of your plate should be whole grains such as rice, quinoa, wheat berries, or barley.

Drink in moderation. Mediterranean philosophy suggests wine in moderation, although I personally enjoy an alcohol-free lifestyle and it's easy to get the benefits of wine in even healthier ways. Whatever you choose, keep an eye on moderation and be sure to hydrate with plenty of water.

Dessert in moderation. I love a bite of dark chocolate or a spoonful of Chocolate Hummus (page 124) after a meal to really feel satisfied. Again, moderation is key. If you're getting plenty of exercise and eating your veggies, grab a piece of Pistachio Baklava (page 125) and enjoy every bite!

SHOULD I BE WORRIED ABOUT GETTING ENOUGH IRON?

I personally went from being anemic (as an ovo-lacto vegetarian) to having high levels of iron upon going vegan. This makes perfect sense when we note that meat is high in iron whereas dairy products contain zero iron. Therefore, it's common for people to experience a drop in iron when they give up meat and substitute lots of dairy (hi, 19-year-old me who loved cheese blintzes). However, when the iron-free dairy foods are dropped, it becomes easy to get plenty of iron through plants. For example, sesame, beans (and lentils), leafy greens, and tofu are all very rich in iron, just to name a few.

WHAT ABOUT B$_{12}$?

The only supplement I personally advocate for on a healthy vegan diet is vitamin B$_{12}$, although I recommend that for everyone, omnivores included. Vitamin B$_{12}$ is stored in the body for long periods of time, so a daily supplement isn't necessary. However, eating fortified nutritional yeast on a regular basis (my personal and tasty approach) or taking an occasional B$_{12}$ supplement is a good safety precaution.

HOW DO I GET ENOUGH PROTEIN IF I EAT A STRICTLY VEGAN DIET?

The question we *should* be asking is: "How can I avoid excess protein, since it's so detrimental to my health?" Protein is important, but Americans are obsessed with it, even though excess amounts can damage our health, resulting in calcium loss, kidney damage, and liver damage. The Recommended Dietary Allowance (RDA) issued by the Food and Nutrition Board of the

NUTRIENT	DAILY RECOMMENDED INTAKE	GOOD SOURCES
Vitamin B$_{12}$	1 to 25 mcg	Nutritional yeast fortified with B$_{12}$
Vitamin D	400 to 800 IU (10 to 20 mcg)	Vitamin D–fortified products
Iron	19.3 to 20.5 mg for men; 17.0 to 18.9 mg for women	Legumes, green vegetables
Omega-3s	250 to 500 mg	Nuts, seeds (sesame, chia, hemp), legumes, olive oil, sea vegetables, edamame

Institute of Medicine states that we should take in 0.36 grams of protein for every pound that we weigh, or roughly 10 to 12 percent of our daily calorie intake. In contrast, the average American gets almost 16 percent of their calories from protein. All that being said, nutritional needs differ from person to person, and you should always consult your doctor to determine your personal needs.

ALL ABOUT OIL

Olive oil is integral to a Mediterranean diet, but there's some debate as to whether it has a place in a healthy vegan diet. Here's my take: Using oils in moderation—in other words, striving for balance—is key. If we eliminate oils completely, it can render our food dry and bland, which ultimately feels unsatisfying. If we use too much, it can mean excess fat in our diet, which is also less than ideal.

The recipes in this book are aimed at finding that healthy middle ground—just enough, but not too much. And here are the oils I recommend:

Olive oil: This, of course, is the classic Mediterranean oil, and is high in healthy monounsaturated fat, and low in saturated fats. If you use extra-virgin olive oil (which is the least refined, healthiest kind), be prepared for your food to taste like olives. I also recommend using olive oil spray instead of traditional nonstick cooking spray, as it contains healthier fats.

Avocado oil: If you'd prefer your food *not* to taste like olives, this is a good alternative. It's made from the flesh around the pit (not the pit itself) and has an unusually high smoke point, which lends itself to safely cooking at higher temperatures.

Sunflower oil: Another neutral-flavored oil, sunflower is my go-to as it can withstand high temperatures and is heart healthy.

LIFESTYLE PRINCIPLES

Although diet is of utmost importance, if we really want to be vibrantly healthy and happy, we must incorporate other elements of well-being—not unlike our friends in the blue zones (see page 7)! The overall *lifestyle* (not just diet) of the Mediterranean is key to what makes the region so healthy. Adopting a similar lifestyle will help us take our wellness to a whole new level.

Here are some of the keys to living a thriving, Mediterranean-inspired lifestyle:

Don't deprive yourself. Yes, it's great to keep an eye on portions and eat a diet that's low in sweets, fats, and decadent foods. However, feeling deprived is simply not sustainable. Again, balance is absolutely key. Make sure to regularly include enjoyable, satisfying foods (and occasional treats) so that your healthy diet is truly something you can maintain for the rest of your life.

Strive for a calm, happy attitude. At one point in my life, I had a healthy body, but I was filled with anxiety and depression. That's not true health. After improving my state of inner wellness, I was able to enjoy whole-person health and well-being—and that's what I wish for you as well. Some ways to increase your happiness levels include daily meditation, affirmations, positive visualization, and self-reflection. It takes a bit of work, but the payoffs are truly endless.

Make time for family and friends. We often get so wrapped up in work that we don't spend enough time with the people we love. It's important to foster the social connections that nourish us, and one fun way to do that is to have more meals with your friends and family. Mediterranean potluck, anyone?

Move your body more. You don't have to go from couch potato to marathon athlete over-night, but if you take steps (figurative and literal) daily to improve your level of fitness, you'll be surprised at how much healthier, stronger, and more energized you feel. I highly recommend finding types of exercise you love (or, at least, like) and emphasizing those, because you'll be much more likely to do them regularly and stick with them long-term. I like to rotate strengthening exercises with cardio, and try to include a little stretching or yoga daily. And I look forward to them all, because I've found ways to make them fun!

Be mindful. Both in food and in life, creating more awareness is a powerful thing. In fact, you can use your plate as a wonderful mindfulness tool. I recommend being fully present with your food as often as possible, and enjoying it more—really, truly tasting every bite. Aim to chew your food more slowly and stop before you're full, ideally when you've just reached the point of no longer being hungry (versus stopping when your stomach feels full). You'll

CITY LIVING, COUNTRY EATING

When you think about Mediterranean life, you may picture a countryside, resplendent with gardens and fresh food markets on the streets. But if you're an urban-dwelling human, you may wonder how to translate that vibrant, fresh foodie life to your area. I'm here to tell you that you can definitely do it! Here are five ways to make your urban lifestyle feel more Mediterranean:

1. **Find a local farmers' market.** Aim to go once a week—you'll be amazed what you'll find (and who you'll meet) there. I fell in love with farmers' markets as a child (I'd go every Saturday with my grandma), and that love is still going strong decades later.

2. **Look for seasonal ingredients.** Even at regular grocery stores, you can find seasonal ingredients much of the year. Opt for what's local and in season whenever possible.

3. **Choose organic foods.** Whenever possible, go for organic foods, whether you're shopping at a grocery store or a farmers' market. Refer to the charts on pages 137 for more information on which items are especially important to choose organic due to high pesticide levels.

4. **Grow your own food.** You'd be surprised at what you can grow, even if you live in an apartment in the city. Urban gardening is awesome, and there are lots of resources out there to help you create a small yet booming garden without much space. You can also grow food indoors. Nutrient-dense sprouts, microgreens, and fresh herbs grow easily indoors, year-round, no matter where you live.

5. **Sign up for a CSA.** See if there is a CSA (community supported agriculture) service where you live. It's a beautiful (and oh-so-fun) thing to get a weekly goodie box of fresh, organic produce, and it's often at a very reasonable price.

be amazed at how this simple practice can shift your eating habits (and overall health) without much additional effort.

Embrace your inner chef. People often say they don't like cooking, or don't have time. However, I often find that those same people end up loving the art of cooking when they approach it differently and make a few tweaks. Eating at home is healthier, but it's also an act of self-love—and love for your friends and family who eat with you. And there is always time for love! Begin by finding a few recipes you adore and grow your repertoire from there. Hitting up a local farmers' market, growing your own herbs, or taking a cooking class can also be great ways to increase the food love in your life!

THE VEGAN MEDITERRANEAN KITCHEN

Are you getting excited to start cooking up delicious, healthy meals in your kitchen? I sure hope so! But first, you'll need a few tools. I've found that having a well-set-up kitchen with a few key extras makes a world of difference because you won't have any obstacles in the way when it comes to preparing fabulous meals. I've also noticed there are a lot of unnecessary gadgets on the market today. *Banana slicer, anyone?* I'm here to help you discern between what's superfluous (and likely a waste of money) and what really *will* help you make cooking a (Mediterranean) breeze.

Must-Have Equipment

If you don't already have the following pieces in your kitchen, I highly encourage you to invest! When you have the right tools, cooking at home becomes much easier—and thus all the more joyous.

Pots and pans: Having a couple of reliable pots and pans to choose from is a necessity. I prefer stainless steel for my pots and have both small and large sizes. For my pans, I recommend cast iron and nonstick, and it's helpful to have a few different sizes there as well. I use these daily, and the bigger the better (even a wok works well for lots of dishes). There are lots of nontoxic nonstick pans on the market today, and they don't need to cost a fortune. Be sure to wash by hand and air-dry to preserve the surface.

Blender: If possible, invest in a high-speed blender (such as Vitamix or Blendtec), as it's worth its weight in gold. These types of blenders typically last a lifetime, so they more than pay for themselves. You'll use a high-speed blender for lots of the smoothie, sauce, and soup recipes in this book.

Chef's knife: In case you don't already have a good chef's knife, I want to give you a gentle nudge here. Having a really sharp, well-designed chef's knife is life-changing. I've known people who think they can't cook, but it's really because they're using a sad little knife. You don't need to spend a fortune—I've had my Victorinox knife for ages and it still works wonderfully. Other brands such as Henckels and Shun also have good chef's knives. Be sure to keep yours out of the dishwasher and sharpen it every few months (either at home with a good sharpener or at a local sharpening service).

Measuring cups and spoons: These are basic (and cheap) as can be, but almost every kitchen I visit is shockingly low on them. If you want to really dig in to cooking (and this cookbook), it will make your life easier to have several sets of these on hand. Plus, you can pop them in the dishwasher. Easy-peasy!

Food processor: This isn't an everyday item, but it's really handy to have when you're making more of your own food from scratch! For this book, you'll want to have a food processor to make Raspberry Cheesecake Squares (page 132), Macadamia-Rosemary Cheese (page 27), and similar treats. Be sure to locate a good model, as the cheap ones (under $100) tend to be flimsy and don't blend very well. The components of a food processor all go in a dishwasher, which makes cleanup easy.

Nice-to-Have Equipment

Although you don't need to own the following tools, they would definitely come in handy for the recipes in this book. Yes, I use a lot of garlic and lemons!

Garlic press: We're all garlic lovers here, right? Having a really good garlic press will make your garlic-lovin' life so much easier. For extra time savings, I use a Pampered Chef model that doesn't require me to peel the cloves. It even comes with a little tool to make cleanup easier. Wash your garlic press by hand and air-dry.

Citrus juicer: I use both an electric juicer and a handheld one, as they work well in different circumstances. Find one that you like and you'll be juicing up lemons and limes in far less time than it takes to do by hand.

Citrus zester: The grated zest of limes, lemons, and oranges can make a dish sing. I use a Microplane for this purpose, and when I'm done I simply rinse it and let it air-dry.

Mandoline: If you like the texture of julienne-cut carrots, uniformly shaped French fries, or paper-thin cucumber slices, this handy tool will become your new best friend. Be sure to use the hand guard for safety and rinse when you're done, allowing it to air-dry.

SPICE UP YOUR PANTRY

If you want to add some zing to your panty with fun new Mediterranean flavors, you'll find that these options are a great place to start:

Harissa: This Tunisian hot pepper paste is usually more flavorful than spicy. It can be found at Trader Joe's, online, or at specialty markets. You'll use it to make Harissa Tofu (page 30) and it's also a great way to wake up plain vegetables or grains.

Tahini: This "butter" results from grinding up sesame seeds. It varies in thickness, so you may want to experiment to find your favorite brand. It's available in any grocery store, health food store, or international market. It's a key ingredient in Happy Hummus (page 23), Classic Baba Ghanoush (page 22), and Easy Tahini-Herb Dressing (page 26).

Za'atar: A sublimely delicious spice blend, za'atar is made from tangy sumac, sesame seeds, and spices. You can find it in specialty stores and online, and you'll use it in the Za'atar Crisps (page 64), Fattoush Salad (page 78), and other dishes.

Pomegranate Molasses: This sweet-tart syrup is a delicious base for sauces and dressings and can be purchased online or at some international markets.

Aleppo Pepper: This pepper from Turkey has a mild heat and a slightly fruity flavor. You can find it at specialty stores and some major supermarkets. It's a fun, Mediterranean swap for red pepper flakes or pink peppercorns.

ABOUT THE RECIPES

The vibrant recipes in this book follow the dietary guidelines we talked about earlier, as they contain mostly whole foods and are plant based, high in nutrients, and low in saturated fats and sugars. They're also meant to make your transition to a vegan Mediterranean diet as fun, easy, and delicious as possible. Here's what to expect:

Meals made simple: Most of the recipes in this book take 30 minutes or less, require only one pot or pan (or a blender), or have fewer than 10 ingredients. I find there's nothing more frustrating in a recipe than unnecessary steps, so I've made these as simple as possible, while still maintaining the integrity and flavor of each recipe. This way it'll be even easier for you to adopt a healthy, happy way of eating that you'll want to stick with for life.

Dietary labels: You'll see any or all of the following dietary labels with each recipe: gluten-free, nut-free, oil-free, and soy-free. Keep in mind, these labels are not an endorsement (or judgment) of these ingredients. Personally, I eat gluten, nuts, oil, and soy (although usually in moderation). However, these labels will make it easy to quickly pick out recipes that work for your dietary preferences.

A range of countries: The recipes in this book come from various countries in the Mediterranean—Greece, Southern Italy, Spain, Turkey, Israel, Cyprus, Portugal, Morocco, Southern France, Croatia, Lebanon, and Syria. Regardless of the differences among these cultures, their traditional cuisines share very similar foundations—they are heavily plant based, high in monounsaturated fat and low in saturated fats, and they feature plenty of omega-3 fatty acids, loads of legumes and whole grains, and lots of vibrant vegetables and fruits. These common threads form the fabric of what's known as the Mediterranean diet.

Fusion for fun: These recipes predominantly feature Mediterranean recipes and flavors, but who doesn't want to mix it up every now and then? Occasionally you'll see a recipe that's been bumped up a notch with some Japanese- or Mexican-inspired flavors.

Bold flavors: A healthy diet is one thing, but a scrumptious healthy diet? That's quite another. In this book, you'll find recipes with bold, bright flavors thanks to lots of lemon, garlic, and love—and just the right amount of salt and spices as well.

Ready to get cooking?

FUL MEDAMES, P. 31

STAPLES

CLASSIC BABA GHANOUSH

GLUTEN-FREE, NUT-FREE, SOY-FREE   **SERVES 4 TO 6**   **PREP TIME: 10 MINUTES / COOK TIME: 40 MINUTES**

Baba ghanoush—fun to say, but even more fun to eat! This creamy dip originated in Levantine (that is, Eastern Mediterranean) cuisine. If you think you dislike baba ghanoush because you've tried it before and found it bitter or bland, I implore (yes, implore) you to try it again. This recipe has a few secrets in it that will leave you with a creamy and delectable dip that's surprisingly easy to make. For example, did you know you don't have to peel the eggplant? Time saver! Also, squeezing the moisture out of the eggplant is a step most people miss, but it works wonders to remove bitterness, resulting in a creamy, dreamy dip or spread.

¼ cup olive oil, plus more for greasing

1 medium eggplant

6 tablespoons freshly squeezed lemon juice

¼ cup tahini

4 garlic cloves, peeled

1 teaspoon sea salt

1. Preheat the oven to 400°F. Lightly grease a rimmed baking sheet with olive oil.

2. Cut the eggplant in half lengthwise. Place the halves, cut-side down, on the sheet and bake for 40 minutes, or until very tender. Set aside to cool.

3. Once cool, squeeze all the moisture out of the eggplant by wringing each half with your hands over the sink. You should end up with about 2 cups smushed eggplant.

4. Remove the stem and place the smushed eggplant (skin and all) in a food processor or blender. Add the olive oil, lemon juice, tahini, garlic, and salt. Blend until smooth, 1 to 2 minutes. The blending time might seem long, but it's well worth it for the creamy, rich result.

5. Serve immediately or store in an airtight container in the refrigerator for up to 1 week.

Serving Tip: Serve cold or at room temperature, alongside some fresh Pita Bread (page 65), Za'atar Crisps (page 64), pita chips, crackers, or raw vegetables for dipping. You can also top the baba ghanoush with one or more or of the following: chopped fresh flat-leaf parsley, Kalamata olives, roasted pine nuts, or a drizzle of olive oil.

Per Serving: Calories: 235; Total Fat: 21g; Saturated Fat: 3g; Protein: 4g; Carbs: 11g; Fiber: 6g; Sodium: 492mg; Iron: 2mg

HAPPY HUMMUS

GLUTEN-FREE, NUT-FREE, SOY-FREE   **SERVES 6**   **PREP TIME: 5 MINUTES**

To me, hummus is the epitome of food happiness, especially when it's homemade and delicious—like this version! It's the perfect staple for dipping—scoop it up with Pita Bread (page 65), crackers, or raw vegetables, adding to sandwiches, and even making a Greek-inspired pizza. It's also packed with protein from the chickpeas and nutrients from the immune-boosting lemon and garlic. So much happiness in one humble dish! Please note that as with many dishes that include raw garlic, this may taste strong at first, but the flavors will mellow out and marry perfectly when allowed to rest in the fridge overnight.

1 (15-ounce) can chickpeas *or* 1½ cups cooked chickpeas, rinsed and drained, 2 tablespoons canning or cooking liquid reserved

2 or 3 garlic cloves, peeled

6 tablespoons freshly squeezed lemon juice

¼ cup tahini

¼ cup olive oil

½ teaspoon sea salt, plus more as needed

1. In a blender or food processor, blend the chickpeas, reserved liquid, and garlic for about 1 minute until relatively smooth.

2. Add the lemon juice, tahini, olive oil, and salt and blend until velvety smooth. If desired, add up to ½ teaspoon additional salt. For best results, refrigerate overnight and allow to warm to room temperature before serving. Store in an airtight container in the refrigerator for up to 1 week.

Ingredient Tip: I'm often asked if it's okay to substitute bottled lemon juice or jarred minced garlic. I highly recommend you don't do that. There's just nothing like fresh lemon and garlic for a bright, authentic flavor and optimal nutrients. And you don't want anything less than full-on happiness, right?

Per Serving: Calories: 255; Total Fat: 16g; Saturated Fat: 2g; Protein: 8g; Carbs: 22g; Fiber: 6g; Sodium: 175mg; Iron: 3mg

VIBRANT BEET HUMMUS

GLUTEN-FREE, NUT-FREE, SOY-FREE   SERVES 6   PREP TIME: 10 MINUTES / COOK TIME: 20 MINUTES

This twist on classic hummus is an absolute stunner. It has just enough beet to be a glorious shade of pink—but not so much that it tastes overly earthy or sweet. As such, it's perfection for parties or special events, when you really want to impress your guests with something healthy, yet pretty and delicious. I like to serve this hummus cold or at room temperature with crackers, raw vegetables, Za'atar Crisps (page 64), or Pita Bread (page 65).

Olive oil cooking spray

1 small beet, peeled and finely diced (about 1 cup chopped beet)

1 (15-ounce) can chickpeas *or* 1½ cups cooked chickpeas, rinsed and drained, ½ cup canning or cooking liquid reserved

5 tablespoons freshly squeezed lime juice

¼ cup tahini

1 tablespoon olive oil

3 garlic cloves, peeled

½ teaspoon sea salt

1.   Preheat the oven to 400°F. Spray a rimmed baking sheet with cooking spray.

2.   Scatter the beet cubes on the prepared sheet. Spray the tops lightly with cooking spray and bake until very tender, about 20 minutes.

3.   Transfer the beet cubes to a blender or food processor and add the chickpeas and reserved liquid, lime juice, tahini, olive oil, garlic, and salt. Blend until the mixture is velvety smooth. Serve immediately or store in an airtight container in the refrigerator for up to 1 week.

Love Your Leftovers: If you've got extra lime juice on hand, there are lots of great uses for it—in fact, I'm always hoping I'll have extra. It's great in water (or with sparkling water and a dash of stevia for sparkling limeade) for an alkalinizing drink. It also freezes very well and is great to keep on hand for future use that way. However, since I use mine fairly quickly, it can just be refrigerated in an airtight container, preferably glass, for up to 1 week. From there, sprinkle it on avocado toast, tacos, or salads.

Per Serving: Calories: 208; Total Fat: 10g; Saturated Fat: 1g; Protein: 8g; Carbs: 25g; Fiber: 7g; Sodium: 186mg; Iron: 3mg

TANGY CHEESE DIP

GLUTEN-FREE, OIL-FREE, SOY-FREE **SERVES 4** **PREP TIME: 10 MINUTES**

This cheesy dip may not be 100 percent Mediterranean, but it's totally vegan and totally delicious—and also high in fiber and low in fat. Use it in many of the wraps and sandwiches in chapter 5, or just plain as a dip for raw cucumbers, celery, crackers, or Za'atar Crisps (page 64). If you don't have a high-speed blender, soak the cashews for a few hours beforehand, then drain them before using so that they're soft enough to blend smooth.

1 (15-ounce) can white beans *or* 1½ cups cooked white beans, rinsed and drained

¼ cup nutritional yeast

¼ cup raw unsalted cashew pieces (see headnote)

¼ cup roasted red peppers

2 tablespoons freshly squeezed lemon juice

2 tablespoons water

2 garlic cloves, peeled

½ teaspoon sea salt

1. In a blender, combine the beans, yeast, cashews, roasted red peppers, lemon juice, water, garlic, and salt. Blend for about 1 minute until very smooth and velvety.

2. Serve cold or at room temperature. Store leftovers in an airtight container in the refrigerator for up to 1 week.

Per Serving: Calories: 257; Total Fat: 5g; Saturated Fat: 1g; Protein: 20g; Carbs: 37g; Fiber: 11g; Sodium: 275mg; Iron: 5mg

EASY TAHINI-HERB DRESSING

GLUTEN-FREE, NUT-FREE, OIL-FREE, SOY-FREE   **MAKES ABOUT 2½ CUPS**   **PREP TIME: 5 MINUTES**

This scrumptious, brightly flavored dressing comes together in 5 minutes with items you probably have on hand, so you may find yourself making this a weekly go-to in your home! It's delicious on salads, drizzled over Falafel (page 44) or Lean, Green Protein Pancakes (page 56), and even as an easy way to jazz up simple baked potatoes, steamed veggies, or brown rice. Tahini is a great source of omega-3s, calcium, and iron. Don't you just love it when the foods you love actually love you back?

1 cup tahini

½ to 1 cup water

½ cup freshly squeezed lemon juice

4 garlic cloves, minced

2 tablespoons dried dill

1 tablespoon dried parsley

2 teaspoons onion granules or powder

1½ teaspoons sea salt

1. In a medium bowl, whisk the tahini with ½ cup of water until smooth.

2. Add the lemon juice, garlic, dill, parsley, onion, and salt and whisk well. For thick tahini (like the one I use), you'll need to add up to ½ cup additional water. If your tahini is runny, begin with half that amount (or less) and add more until your desired consistency is reached.

3. Serve immediately or store in an airtight container in the refrigerator for up to 1 week.

Tasty Tip: If you have fresh herbs on hand, by all means use them instead of the dried ones here. This recipe is meant to be super easy for everyday use, but it's even better with fresh herbs. Some that work well here are dill, parsley, chives, and rosemary.

Ingredient Tip: The brand of tahini I typically use is very thick, so I need the full 1 cup of water when I make this dressing. No matter what brand of tahini you use, I recommend an organic version that's made from raw, not roasted, sesame seeds.

Per Serving: Calories: 149; Total Fat: 13g; Saturated Fat: 2g; Protein: 4g; Carbs: 6g; Fiber: 2g; Sodium: 102mg; Iron: 2mg

MACADAMIA-ROSEMARY CHEESE

GLUTEN-FREE, SOY-FREE   **SERVES 6**   **PREP TIME: 10 MINUTES**

Thanks in large part to our fine friend the glorious macadamia nut, this cheese is so darn satisfying you might find it knocks out your cravings for unhealthy snacks altogether. It's also high in good fats, with a large dose of omega-3s. You can use it as a spread for sandwiches, on The Athena Pizza (page 112), as a dip for crackers, or with Za'atar Crisps (page 64). If you don't have a food processor, you can use a blender, but you may need to add additional water or oil to achieve a velvety smooth result.

1 cup raw macadamia nuts

¼ cup water

2 tablespoons nutritional yeast

2 tablespoons extra-virgin olive oil

2 tablespoons freshly squeezed lemon juice

2 garlic cloves, peeled

½ teaspoon sea salt

2 teaspoons dried or chopped fresh rosemary

1. In a food processor, combine the nuts, water, nutritional yeast, olive oil, lemon juice, garlic, and salt and process until completely smooth.

2. Pulse in the rosemary until it's blended into the cheese but still visible (you want to be able to see flecks of green). Transfer the cheese to an airtight container and refrigerate overnight before serving, as the flavors are best when they've had a chance to mellow and marry. Serve cold or at room temperature. Store in an airtight container in the refrigerator for up to 2 weeks.

Ingredient Tip: Macadamia nuts are pricey but worth it. They have a unique, buttery flavor that's very hard to match, so although other soft nuts like cashews could work in this recipe, the result won't taste quite as good. There's no need to soak the macadamias for this recipe, so just toss them into your food processor as is.

Per Serving: Calories: 224; Total Fat: 22g; Saturated Fat: 3g; Protein: 5g; Carbs: 6g; Fiber: 4g; Sodium: 160mg; Iron: 1mg

POMEGRANATE-BALSAMIC REDUCTION

GLUTEN-FREE, NUT-FREE, OIL-FREE, SOY-FREE   MAKES 1¼ CUPS
PREP TIME: 2 MINUTES / COOK TIME: 1 HOUR

This homemade glaze is so fresh and has such depth that you might want to keep it on hand at all times. It's also easy to prepare, despite what may seem like a long cook time. Your actual "baby-sitting" time is minimal, as you'll mostly just be drifting about your house, happily smelling this simmering pot on your stove. Use this reduction as the foundation for Luscious Moroccan Sauce (page 29), or pull it out any time you want to liven up salads, bean and grain dishes, stir-fries, and dressings.

3 cups pomegranate juice

1 cup balsamic vinegar

¾ cup coconut sugar

1 tablespoon freshly squeezed lemon juice

¼ teaspoon sea salt

1. In a medium pot, combine the pomegranate juice, vinegar, coconut sugar, lemon juice, and salt and bring to a boil over medium-high heat, stirring often.

2. Reduce the heat to low. Simmer for 1 hour, whisking every 10 minutes or so.

3. After about an hour, the mixture will be reduced to about 1¼ cups. Watch it carefully at this point, because it will become much more syrupy and start bubbling rapidly. Once this happens, remove the pan from the heat and allow the mixture to cool in the pan.

4. Once cooled, the reduction will thicken up to a molasses consistency. Use immediately or store in an airtight container in the refrigerator for up to 1 month.

Simple Swap: Coconut sugar is much healthier than regular white sugar, and it has a slight hint of caramel flavor (similar to brown sugar). I recommend using it here, but you can also use regular organic white sugar instead if that's what you have on hand, or if you prefer a more traditional flavor.

Per Serving: Calories: 131; Total Fat: 0g; Saturated Fat: 0g; Protein: 0g; Carbs: 32g; Fiber: 0g; Sodium: 64mg; Iron: 0mg

LUSCIOUS MOROCCAN SAUCE

GLUTEN-FREE, NUT-FREE, SOY-FREE   **MAKES ABOUT 1¾ CUPS**
PREP TIME: 10 MINUTES / COOK TIME: 5 MINUTES

This gorgeous sauce is what makes French Lentil Salad (page 82) and Moroccan Tempeh (page 106) so wonderful. It's also just the thing for making a simple salad or grain dish sing. The list of ingredients may look long, but it's mostly just a matter of measuring some stuff into a pot and stirring. Easy-peasy. Even if you're a cooking novice, you'll feel like a champion after whipping up a batch of this sauce!

½ cup Pomegranate-Balsamic Reduction (page 28)

½ cup water

½ cup freshly squeezed orange juice

2 tablespoons freshly squeezed lime juice

2 tablespoons neutral-flavored oil (sunflower, olive, or safflower)

4 teaspoons pure maple syrup

1 teaspoon salt

½ teaspoon ground cinnamon

½ teaspoon ground cumin

¼ teaspoon ground coriander

2 garlic cloves, minced or pressed

2 teaspoons arrowroot powder or cornstarch

1. In a medium saucepan, combine the balsamic reduction, water, orange and lime juices, oil, maple syrup, salt, cinnamon, cumin, coriander, and garlic. Cook over medium heat, whisking often, for 2 to 3 minutes.

2. Transfer about 2 tablespoons of the sauce to a small bowl and stir in the arrowroot until smooth and dissolved. Return the liquid to the saucepan and whisk well.

3. Continue to cook for 1 to 2 minutes, whisking often, until the mixture is just thickened. Remove from the heat and serve hot or warm. Store in an airtight container in the refrigerator for up to 2 weeks.

Per Serving: Calories: 116; Total Fat: 4g; Saturated Fat: 1g; Protein: 0g; Carbs: 21g; Fiber: 0g; Sodium: 363mg; Iron: 0mg

HARISSA TOFU

GLUTEN-FREE, NUT-FREE   SERVES 4   PREP TIME: 10 MINUTES / COOK TIME: 5 MINUTES

This brightly colored tofu is delicious on its own, or in sandwiches, on salads, or as part of an antipasto plate. Although the harissa has a chile base, it's not excessively spicy. However, if you're not a fan of heat in general, you can cut the amount of harissa in half—or, for more heat, add extra harissa or a little kick of cayenne.

1 (14-ounce) package firm or extra-firm tofu

1 teaspoon freshly squeezed lemon juice

2½ tablespoons harissa paste

6 garlic cloves, minced or pressed

2 teaspoons arrowroot or cornstarch

4 teaspoons cornmeal

3 tablespoons olive oil

½ teaspoon sea salt

1. Drain the tofu and cut it crosswise into 8 slabs. Place the slabs on a clean work surface or large plate in a single layer and cover with paper towels or tea towels. Press well (yet gently) to remove excess moisture from the tofu.

2. Cut each slab in half (you should have 16 squares, each about 2 inches in size). Drizzle the lemon juice on top. Spread the harissa paste and garlic evenly on both sides of the tofu. Sprinkle both sides with the arrowroot, and then with the cornmeal.

3. In a large skillet, heat the oil over medium-high heat. When hot, add the tofu in a single layer and sprinkle with the salt. Cook for about 2 minutes until golden brown underneath, then gently flip each piece and cook for another 2 minutes until golden brown and crisp on the other side. Serve immediately.

Ingredient Tip: Harissa is a Tunisian hot pepper paste and can be found at Trader Joe's, international markets, many grocery stores, and online. I've found that the flavor of different harissa pastes varies greatly, so if you don't like one brand, you may love another. Depending on the flavor profile of your favorite brand, you may want to adjust the salt and garlic in this recipe to reflect your desired result.

Per Serving: Calories: 229; Total Fat: 18g; Saturated Fat: 2g; Protein: 11g; Carbs: 9g; Fiber: 1g; Sodium: 357mg; Iron: 2mg

FUL MEDAMES

GLUTEN-FREE, NUT-FREE, SOY-FREE   SERVES 5   PREP TIME: 10 MINUTES

This classic Egyptian bean dish is incredibly simple to make yet overflowing with vibrant flavor. I love it immensely for those reasons and also because it's so nutrient dense. The beans are a great source of iron, fiber, and protein, and the abundance of fresh lemon gives your body a cleansing, alkalinizing boost. And as a bonus, the parsley and garlic are both immune boosting and detoxifying. This healthy dish is on regular rotation in our house—even picky kids tend to love it! We serve it with Happy Hummus (page 23), Za'atar Crisps (page 64), and Catalonian Kale Salad (page 85) for a flavor-filled, nutrient-packed meal.

2 (15-ounce) cans fava beans *or* 3 cups cooked fava beans, rinsed and drained

1 small tomato, chopped

¼ cup minced fresh flat-leaf parsley

3½ tablespoons freshly squeezed lemon juice

1½ tablespoons extra-virgin olive oil

2 garlic cloves, minced or pressed

¾ teaspoon sea salt

In a large bowl, combine the beans, tomato, parsley, lemon juice, olive oil, garlic, and salt and mix well. Serve at room temperature or cold. Store in an airtight container in the refrigerator for up to 1 week.

Ingredient Swap: If you're unable to find canned fava beans, you can substitute white beans (cannellini), pinto beans, or gigante beans. And if you're not a fan of parsley, feel free to use cilantro or minced spinach instead.

Per Serving: Calories: 229; Total Fat: 5g; Saturated Fat: 1g; Protein: 13g; Carbs: 35g; Fiber: 10g; Sodium: 294mg; Iron: 3mg

LEMONY GRILLED ARTICHOKES, P. 46

3

SMALL PLATES AND SNACKS

DELICIOUS DOLMAS

GLUTEN-FREE, NUT-FREE, SOY-FREE   **SERVES 7**   **PREP TIME: 20 MINUTES / COOK TIME: 50 MINUTES**

Please don't be intimidated by the idea of making stuffed grape leaves at home—these flavorful little beauties are easy to make and very forgiving while you're still learning. I love making them from scratch because they're less likely to be oily (they're usually soaking in oil in restaurants and olive bars), plus this recipe is extra nourishing from the brown rice and other whole-food ingredients. You can make the filling in advance and store it in the fridge until you're ready to roll. Serve with Happy Hummus (page 23) or Vibrant Beet Hummus (page 24), Classic Baba Ghanoush (page 22), Falafel (page 44), and Quinoa Tabbouleh (page 80) for a full-on Greek feast!

½ cup long-grain brown rice

1 cup water

2 Roma tomatoes, finely chopped

1½ tablespoons extra-virgin olive oil

2 tablespoons freshly squeezed lemon juice

2 tablespoons finely minced onion

1½ tablespoons minced fresh flat-leaf parsley

1 teaspoon dried dill

¼ teaspoon sea salt

1 (16-ounce) jar grape leaves

1. Combine the rice and water in a small pot and bring to a boil over high heat. Reduce the heat to low, cover, and simmer until the rice is tender and all the water is absorbed, about 30 minutes. Uncover and set aside to cool for 5 minutes.

2. Stir the rice and add the tomatoes, olive oil, lemon juice, onion, parsley, dill, and salt. Stir gently, just until well combined with the rice.

3. Place a steamer insert in a large pot with a tight-fitting lid. Add a little water to the pot, being careful not to bring the water level above the bottom of the insert. Set aside.

4. Gently remove a cluster of leaves from the jar. Place one grape leaf on a clean work surface, smooth-side down, with the stem base closest to you.

5. Place 1 tablespoon of the filling in the center of the leaf. Fold the bottom of the grape leaf up and over the filling. Next, fold in the sides. Finally, roll up from the bottom to form a cigar-shaped dolma. Place it in the steamer with the seam-side down.

6. Repeat until the rice mixture is used up—you should get about 28 dolmas. Cover the pot and steam over medium heat for 20 minutes, or until the grape leaves become tender. Remove from the heat and allow to cool for at least 5 minutes. Serve warm or cold. Store in an airtight container in the refrigerator for up to 3 days.

Technique Tip: Since the salt content in grape leaves varies, it's best to make the rice mixture less salty than you'd normally prefer.

Ingredient Tip: You can find jars of preserved grape leaves in most supermarkets these days, but, when in doubt, stop by your local Mediterranean/Middle Eastern food market.

Per Serving: Calories: 97; Total Fat: 4g; Saturated Fat: 1g; Protein: 2g; Carbs: 14g; Fiber: 2g; Sodium: 429mg; Iron: 1mg

GARLICKY MUSHROOMS

NUT-FREE   **SERVES 4**   **PREP TIME: 5 MINUTES / COOK TIME: 10 MINUTES**

These tasty mushrooms are simple yet oddly enticing. There's something about the seasonings here that really coax the flavor out of mushrooms. I use portobellos for this recipe, but any kind of mushroom will work beautifully—shiitakes, cremini, and even plain old humble button mushrooms. All varieties of mushrooms are little rock stars because they lend a meaty satisfaction yet are low in calories (and, of course, cholesterol free) and high in B vitamins, potassium, and antioxidants.

1 pound portobello mushrooms

2 tablespoons olive oil

1½ tablespoons balsamic vinegar

1½ tablespoons tamari, shoyu, or soy sauce

6 garlic cloves, minced or pressed

½ teaspoon dried or minced fresh rosemary

Salt (optional)

Freshly ground black pepper (optional)

1. Discard the mushroom stems, slice the caps, and put them in a large skillet.

2. Add the olive oil, vinegar, and tamari to the skillet and sauté over medium-high heat for 5 minutes, stirring often, until the mushrooms begin to brown and soften.

3. Add the garlic and rosemary, stir, and sauté for another 5 minutes, or until the mushrooms are tender and look caramelized. Remove the skillet from the heat. Season with salt and pepper (if using). Serve warm.

Love Your Leftovers: Do you feel bad about tossing those mushroom stems? I can relate. Here's what I do when I have leftover bits and pieces from flavorful veggies: I toss them in a freezer bag and store them in the freezer. Once my bag is full, I cook the veggie scraps in a pot of water for a few hours to extract the flavors. Then, I strain off the liquid and use it whenever I want a richly flavored vegetable broth to use for soups, sauces, or grains. My favorite flavorful broth-makers include mushroom stems, onion peels and ends, garlic bits and peels, celery and carrot ends, and scallion tops.

Per Serving: Calories: 106; Total Fat: 7g; Saturated Fat: 1g; Protein: 4g; Carbs: 9g; Fiber: 2g; Sodium: 386mg; Iron: 1mg

CUCUMBERS IN TAHINI-DILL SAUCE

GLUTEN-FREE, NUT-FREE, SOY-FREE   **SERVES 4**   **PREP TIME: 10 MINUTES**

There's nothing better than a simple vegetable dish with loads of flavor. Here you have the humble cucumber and onion, made more fabulous with the addition of a flavorful, rich tahini sauce. Keep in mind as you make this recipe that different brands of tahini vary greatly in thickness. You may not need to add additional water if your tahini is runny. If yours is very thick (like the one I used to create this recipe), you'll make this with the additional 2 tablespoons water. Enjoy this salad as a side or small plate as part of a light Mediterranean meal.

2 tablespoons tahini

2 tablespoons freshly squeezed lemon juice

1 tablespoon olive oil

½ teaspoon sea salt

1 to 2 tablespoons water (optional)

2 medium cucumbers or 1 large English cucumber, thinly sliced

1 small red onion, thinly sliced

1 tablespoon minced fresh dill *or* 1 teaspoon dried dill

1. In a large bowl, whisk together the tahini, lemon juice, olive oil, and salt. If the mixture is too thick, add up to 2 tablespoons water and whisk.

2. Once the dressing is smooth and no lumps of tahini remain, add the cucumber, onion, and dill. Stir well, coating the vegetables evenly with the sauce. Serve immediately or store in an airtight container in the refrigerator for up to 4 days. Serve cold or at room temperature.

Per Serving: Calories: 110; Total Fat: 7g; Saturated Fat: 1g; Protein: 2g; Carbs: 8g; Fiber: 2g; Sodium: 247mg; Iron: 1mg

LEMONY POTATOES

GLUTEN-FREE, NUT-FREE, SOY-FREE   SERVES 4   PREP TIME: 5 MINUTES / COOK TIME: 1 HOUR

These full-flavored potatoes are absolutely delicious—there's something about the combination of lemon, garlic, and potatoes that just sends me. Serve them as a side dish or as a component of a main meal alongside Classic Baba Ghanoush (page 22) or Happy Hummus (page 23) and some Pita Bread (page 65) or Za'atar Crisps (page 64). Although I usually don't peel potatoes, I do for this recipe—exposing the flesh of the potatoes allows them to soak up all the heavenly flavors.

5 cups peeled, chopped russet potatoes

3 tablespoons olive, sunflower, or avocado oil, divided

1 teaspoon grated lemon zest

2 tablespoons freshly squeezed lemon juice

3 garlic cloves, minced or pressed

¾ teaspoon sea salt

¼ teaspoon freshly ground black pepper

3 tablespoons minced fresh chives or scallions

1. Preheat the oven to 400°F.

2. Put the potatoes in a 9-by-13-inch baking dish, drizzle with 2 tablespoons of oil, and toss to combine. Bake for 40 minutes, stirring the potatoes two or three times. I use a metal spatula and scrape up from the bottom of the pan so that they brown evenly.

3. Sprinkle on the remaining 1 tablespoon of oil, lemon zest and juice, garlic, salt, and pepper and toss to coat. Bake for 10 minutes, stir, and bake for a final 10 minutes, or until the potatoes are nicely browned and the liquids have been absorbed.

4. Toss with the chives and serve immediately.

Love Your Leftovers: If you have extra chives or scallions, feel free to mince them and store them in the fridge for a few days. If you have them all chopped up and ready to go, you'll be more likely to remember to use them in time. They're great on baked potatoes, tossed with tofu or beans, as a garnish for any of the dips in this book, or on salads.

Per Serving: Calories: 224; Total Fat: 11g; Saturated Fat: 2g; Protein: 3g; Carbs: 30g; Fiber: 5g; Sodium: 14mg; Iron: 1mg

TAHINI CAULIFLOWER WITH CARAMELIZED ONIONS

GLUTEN-FREE, NUT-FREE, SOY-FREE   **SERVES 4**   **PREP TIME: 10 MINUTES / COOK TIME: 30 MINUTES**

This dish is rich, delicious, and such a pretty color. It's also a great source of fiber, antioxidants, and immune-boosting properties. If you like things a bit spicy, be sure to add the harissa paste as it'll kick things up a notch. However, this rosy-colored dish is still full of flavor without it, so have no fear if you find yourself harissa-less at the moment. For a glorious meal, serve this with Spanakopita (page 41) and The Vegan Greek (page 79).

4 cups cauliflower florets

2 teaspoons olive oil

1 small onion, thinly sliced

2 tablespoons tahini

1½ tablespoons tomato paste

2 tablespoons freshly squeezed lemon juice

4 garlic cloves, minced or pressed

2 teaspoons onion granules or powder

½ teaspoon sea salt

1 to 2 tablespoons water (optional)

1 tablespoon harissa paste (optional)

1. Preheat the oven to 400°F.

2. Spread the cauliflower florets in a single layer on a rimmed baking sheet and roast, stirring once, until lightly browned, 20 to 30 minutes. Set aside.

3. In a skillet, heat the oil over medium heat. Sauté the onion for 10 to 20 minutes until the onion is caramelized (very soft and very browned). Set aside.

4. In a large bowl, whisk together the tahini, tomato paste, lemon juice, garlic, onion granules, and salt until smooth. If your tahini is thick, you will need to add the full 2 tablespoons water; if your tahini is thin, you may not need any water at all. Whisk in your desired amount of water and the harissa (if using).

5. Add the cooked cauliflower and onions to the sauce and toss well. Serve.

Per Serving: Calories: 108; Total Fat: 7g; Saturated Fat: 1g; Protein: 4g; Carbs: 11g; Fiber: 4g; Sodium: 281mg; Iron: 1mg

MOROCCAN-SPICED SWEET POTATO FRIES

GLUTEN-FREE, NUT-FREE, SOY-FREE   **SERVES 4**   **PREP TIME: 10 MINUTES / COOK TIME: 25 MINUTES**

Morocco's sweet-savory spices of cumin, paprika, and cinnamon work so beautifully with sweet potatoes in this recipe. These fries are delicious on their own, but you could also serve them with some Luscious Moroccan Sauce (page 29) if you're feeling fancy. You can also serve them alongside Falafel Salad (page 86) or French Lentil Salad (page 82) for a satisfying meal.

4 teaspoons sunflower or avocado oil, plus more for greasing

2 medium sweet potatoes, scrubbed and cut into ¼-inch-thick fries

1 tablespoon coconut sugar or agave nectar

1½ teaspoons ground cinnamon

1½ teaspoons ground cumin

½ teaspoon paprika

½ teaspoon sea salt

¼ teaspoon garlic granules or powder

1½ tablespoons freshly squeezed lime juice

1. Preheat the oven to 400°F. Lightly grease a rimmed baking sheet with oil.

2. In a medium bowl, toss together the sweet potatoes, oil, coconut sugar, cinnamon, cumin, paprika, salt, garlic, and lime juice to mix well.

3. Spread the sweet potatoes out on the prepared baking sheet in a single layer and bake for 10 minutes.

4. Remove from the oven and flip each fry over. Bake for another 10 to 15 minutes until browned and tender. Serve immediately.

Technique Tip: If you have a mandoline, you'll be able to create consistently shaped French fries in no time. Set your mandoline to about ¼ inch for a fry that's not too thick or thin.

Per Serving: Calories: 129; Total Fat: 5g; Saturated Fat: 1g; Protein: 2g; Carbs: 21g; Fiber: 4g; Sodium: 275mg; Iron: 3mg

SPANAKOPITA

NUT-FREE   **SERVES 6**   **PREP TIME: 15 MINUTES / COOK TIME: 20 MINUTES**

This dish seems to intimidate people—perhaps partly due to the use of phyllo dough—but it's actually quite easy to make. The savory onion and garlic play so nicely with the lemon, spinach, and Kalamata olives. For extra lusciousness, you can brush the layers of phyllo with olive oil (or vegan butter) instead of using the spray. Either way, these are absolutely delicious, and you may want to make a double (or triple!) batch of the filling so you can keep it on hand for spanakopita happiness all week. Serve with a salad and some Happy Hummus (page 23), Vibrant Beet Hummus (page 24), or Classic Baba Ghanoush (page 22) for a satisfying meal.

Olive oil cooking spray

4 teaspoons extra-virgin olive oil

½ onion, minced

7 ounces firm or extra-firm tofu

5 ounces baby spinach

4 garlic cloves, minced or pressed

8 Kalamata olives, pitted and chopped

3 tablespoons freshly squeezed lemon juice

½ teaspoon sea salt

6 (13-by-18-inch) sheets phyllo dough, thawed overnight in the refrigerator

1. Preheat the oven to 400°F. Spray a rimmed baking sheet with cooking spray.

2. In a large skillet, heat the oil over medium-high heat. Sauté the onion, stirring often, for 5 to 7 minutes until browned.

3. Using your hands, squeeze the moisture from the tofu over the sink, then crumble it into the skillet. Mix with the onion and sauté for 1 minute. Add the spinach, garlic, and olives and cook for about 1 minute until the spinach is just wilted. Remove the skillet from the heat and stir in the lemon juice and salt until thoroughly combined. Set aside.

Continued on next page

4. Remove one sheet of phyllo and place it on a clean, dry surface. Spray with cooking spray. Fold it lengthwise into thirds, spraying each portion of dry phyllo with cooking spray as you fold, so the exposed phyllo continually gets lightly coated with oil. This will give you a flakier result.

5. Place $1/3$ cup of the tofu-spinach mixture at the base of the phyllo rectangle. Fold the bottom of the phyllo up and over the mixture to meet with the side, forming a triangle. Continue to fold up toward the top, closing the sides of the triangle as you go. Place it on the baking sheet and repeat until you have 6 triangles. Spray the tops with cooking spray and bake for 10 to 12 minutes until golden brown. Serve immediately.

Ingredient Tip: When working with phyllo dough, keep the following in mind: (1) Most phyllo comes in large sheets; if your sheets are smaller, just use two. (2) If the phyllo is going to be sitting out for a while, cover it with a damp dish towel. (3) Be gentle when working with phyllo, as it can tear easily. However, if it does tear, just place another sheet on top (or "patch" it with additional phyllo)—no one will ever know!

Serving Tip: Serve with Easy Tahini-Herb Dressing (page 26) spooned on top for a real treat.

Per Serving: Calories: 134; Total Fat: 7g; Saturated Fat: 1g; Protein: 6g; Carbs: 14g; Fiber: 2g; Sodium: 323mg; Iron: 2mg

OLIVE BRUSCHETTA

NUT-FREE, SOY-FREE   SERVES 6   PREP TIME: 5 MINUTES / COOK TIME: 20 MINUTES

I've made these Greek beauties multiple times for special occasions and dinner parties, and they never fail to be a hit (as in, you'll be looking at empty plates in record time). For a fun, tapas-style party, serve these with Classic Baba Ghanoush (page 22), Za'atar Crisps (page 64), Delicious Dolmas (page 34), and Tahini Cauliflower with Caramelized Onions (page 39), and your guests will feel like they're in the Mediterranean.

6 sourdough bread slices

6 garlic cloves, minced or pressed

24 Kalamata olives, pitted and chopped

1 cup marinated artichoke hearts, drained

½ cup thinly sliced marinated sun-dried tomatoes

1½ tablespoons dried rosemary

3 tablespoons extra-virgin olive oil

Sea salt (optional)

1. Preheat the oven to 375°F.

2. Place the bread slices on a rimmed baking sheet and spread the tops evenly with the garlic. Top each piece evenly with olives, artichokes, and tomatoes. Sprinkle the tops with rosemary and drizzle with olive oil. If desired, sprinkle with a little salt.

3. Bake for 10 to 20 minutes until the bread and toppings are lightly browned. Be careful not to overcook or the rosemary will become bitter. Serve immediately.

Simple Swap: If you're gluten free, you can use polenta as a nutritious base for your toppings. To do so, simply purchase a "log" of polenta (plain or rosemary) and slice it into ½-inch-thick rounds. Then, proceed with the recipe just as you would with the bread. The polenta rounds will make more servings because they'll be smaller. Simply give your guests—or yourself—an extra one (or two). Problem solved! You can find polenta logs in the Italian section of the supermarket, health food stores, and Trader Joe's.

Per Serving: Calories: 207; Total Fat: 11g; Saturated Fat: 2g; Protein: 5g; Carbs: 24g; Fiber: 2g; Sodium: 559mg; Iron: 2mg

FALAFEL

GLUTEN-FREE, NUT-FREE, SOY-FREE   **SERVES 4**   **PREP TIME: 10 MINUTES / COOK TIME: 45 MINUTES**

Falafel is international fast food at its best: crispy, satisfying, beautifully spiced, and filling. It can be enjoyed as a Falafel Wrap (page 74), in a Falafel Salad (page 86), or on its own, simply drizzled with tahini dressing. Falafel is typically deep-fried, but in this recipe it's baked to perfection. The (relatively) small amount of oil I call for here still gives a nod to that "fried" flavor. Purists say that it's imperative to begin with dried chickpeas, but I've found this "cheater" method using canned chickpeas to be delicious, and oh-so-easy to whip up.

Olive oil cooking spray

2 (15-ounce) cans chickpeas *or* 3 cups cooked chickpeas, rinsed and drained

5 garlic cloves, minced or pressed

¼ cup dried or ½ cup finely chopped fresh flat-leaf parsley

2 tablespoons cumin seeds

2½ teaspoons ground coriander

6 tablespoons chickpea flour

¾ teaspoon sea salt

½ teaspoon baking powder

2 tablespoons water

2 tablespoons olive oil

1 recipe Easy Tahini-Herb Dressing (page 26), for serving

1. Preheat the oven to 425°F. Spray a large rimmed baking sheet with cooking spray and set aside.

2. In a food processor or blender, pulse the chickpeas until well blended and relatively paste-like, but with a small amount of texture still remaining.

3. Transfer the chickpeas to a large bowl and stir in the garlic, parsley, cumin seeds, and coriander until combined. Stir in the chickpea flour, salt, baking powder, water, and olive oil.

4. Using your hands, form the mixture into 1-inch balls and place them on the baking sheet, leaving a little space in between each falafel. Repeat until you have as many falafel balls as you'd like to eat immediately. Any leftover batter can be stored, covered, in the refrigerator for up to 5 days.

5. Spray the falafel liberally with cooking spray. Bake, flipping the falafel and spraying the tops every 15 minutes, until browned and crisp, about 45 minutes.

6. Remove and serve drizzled with the tahini dressing.

Simple Swap: If you prefer to use less oil, you can omit the oil from the batter and use an additional 2 tablespoons water instead.

Per Serving: Calories: 730; Total Fat: 43g; Saturated Fat: 6g; Protein: 23g; Carbs: 67g; Fiber: 16g; Sodium: 425mg; Iron: 11mg

LEMONY GRILLED ARTICHOKES

NUT-FREE, SOY-FREE   **SERVES 4**   **PREP TIME: 10 MINUTES / COOK TIME: 30 MINUTES**

As I once said to a friend, "There are two kinds of people in this world—those who love artichokes, and those who are wrong." Artichokes are just that good! With references dating back to ancient Greece, the artichoke has long been a delicacy central to Mediterranean cooking. And, bonus—it's nutritious, too. An artichoke has nearly a quarter of your daily requirement of vitamin C, vitamin K, and folate. In this version, artichokes are dipped in garlicky breadcrumbs for extra fun! And if you're gluten free, you can easily swap in gluten-free bread crumbs.

2 large artichokes (or 4 small)

1 lemon, halved

1 cup whole-grain bread crumbs

½ teaspoon grated lemon zest

3 garlic cloves, minced or pressed

4 teaspoons olive oil, divided, plus more for brushing

4 teaspoons lemon juice

¼ teaspoon sea salt, plus more for sprinkling

1. To prepare the artichokes, cut the stem to 1 inch. Slice off the spiky top portion, and, if desired, trim the tips of the remaining leaves with scissors. Cut each artichoke in half from stem to top and rub the cut parts with one lemon half to reduce browning.

2. Place a steamer insert in a large pot with about an inch of water in it and bring to a simmer. Arrange the artichokes in the steamer basket cut-side up, and cover the pot. Steam over medium-low heat for about 20 minutes, or until a knife easily pierces the inside heart of the artichoke and a leaf from the outside pulls away easily. Remove from heat and set aside.

3. While the artichokes are cooking, in a medium skillet, combine the bread crumbs, lemon zest, garlic, 2 teaspoons oil, and ¼ teaspoon salt. Cook over medium heat for 2 to 3 minutes stirring constantly, until golden brown. Remove from heat and set aside.

4. Heat a grill to medium-high heat. Brush the artichokes lightly with oil and place them cut-side down on the grill. Cook for 2 to 3 minutes. Turn the artichokes over and cook for an additional 2 to 3 minutes.

5. Drizzle the artichokes with the remaining 2 teaspoons oil and 4 teaspoons lemon juice. Sprinkle lightly with sea salt. Enjoy the leaves and tender heart and stem portions (discarding any tough and fuzzy parts), dipping them liberally in the breadcrumbs.

Super Easy: If you don't want to fire up the grill, simply omit step four and serve the steamed artichokes drizzled with olive oil and lemon juice and dipped in breadcrumbs. Just as delicious!

Serving Tip: If you want to make this dish even prettier, grill halved lemons alongside the artichokes. Simply cut the lemons in half, brush lightly with olive oil, and grill.

Ingredient Tip: Peak season for artichokes is in the spring, although they're generally available year-round. A fresh artichoke has tightly closed leaves and very few brown spots, and should be heavy for its size.

Per Serving: Calories: 130; Total Fat: 4g; Saturated Fat: 1g; Protein: 5g; Carbs: 20g; Fiber: 5g; Sodium: 238mg; Iron: 2mg

CHOCOLATE DREAM SMOOTHIE BOWL, P. 53

BREAKFASTS

THE BEST VEGAN DATE SHAKE

GLUTEN-FREE, NUT-FREE, OIL-FREE, SOY-FREE   **SERVES 4**   **PREP TIME: 5 MINUTES**

Chickpeas in a milkshake—what the heck? Yes, I hear you. It's almost as weird as Chocolate Hummus (page 124). Chickpeas are an amazing addition to this shake because they will keep you going for hours with their fiber-rich, protein-dense nutritional profile, yet their mild flavor disappears right into the vanilla creaminess. Use this yummy shake as a mini-meal anytime you need a boost.

1 (15-ounce) can chickpeas *or* 1½ cups cooked chickpeas, rinsed and drained

10 pitted dates

1 tablespoon vanilla extract

2¼ cups unsweetened nondairy milk, plus more as needed

3 large frozen bananas

Pinch sea salt (optional)

In a blender, combine the chickpeas, dates, vanilla, nondairy milk, bananas, and salt (if using) and process until completely smooth. If you need more liquid, add a little more nondairy milk and process to combine. Enjoy immediately.

Technique Tip: If you don't have a high-speed blender, soak the dates in the milk for several hours in the refrigerator so they soften enough to blend smooth.

Super Easy: If you want an even easier version of this shake, you can omit the dates and add a dash of sweetener, such as maple syrup, instead.

Per Serving: Calories: 278; Total Fat: 4g; Saturated Fat: 0g; Protein: 7g; Carbs: 56g; Fiber: 9g; Sodium: 118mg; Iron: 3mg

HEMERA'S STRAWBERRY SMOOTHIE

GLUTEN-FREE, OIL-FREE, SOY-FREE   **SERVES 4**   **PREP TIME: 5 MINUTES**

Hemera is the Greek goddess of the daytime, and so is this delicious smoothie. It's easy to prepare, stunning in flavor, and the perfect way to start your day. Serve this on mornings when you need an impressive, satisfying drink to serve guests, or simply make it for yourself when you've got a busy day ahead and need some extra love and nourishment. This drink is packed with fiber, iron, vitamin C, and healthy fats and is perfect for the spirit of joyful Mediterranean living.

3 cups frozen strawberries

2 frozen bananas

¾ cup raw unsalted cashew pieces

12 pitted dates

1 tablespoon vanilla extract

2¼ cups unsweetened nondairy milk, plus more as needed

In a blender, process the strawberries, bananas, cashews, dates, vanilla, and nondairy milk until completely smooth. If you need more liquid, add a little more nondairy milk and process to combine. Serve right away.

Technique Tip: If you don't have a high-speed blender, soak the cashews and dates in water for a few hours beforehand, then drain before using so that they're soft enough to blend smooth.

Super Easy: If desired, try using half the dates for a smoothie that still boasts plenty of fruity sweetness without the extra sugar. Depending on the sweetness of your strawberries, you may find that 6 to 8 dates tastes great to you.

Ingredient Tip: I call for cashew pieces here because they're typically less expensive than whole cashews and are easier to measure. However, if you're using whole cashews, just make sure they're raw (not roasted) and add a smidge more as they'll take up less space in the measuring cup than the pieces.

Per Serving: Calories: 348; Total Fat: 14g; Saturated Fat: 2g; Protein: 7g; Carbs: 50g; Fiber: 8g; Sodium: 206mg; Iron: 2mg

GREEN GAIA SMOOTHIE

GLUTEN-FREE, NUT-FREE, OIL-FREE, SOY-FREE   **SERVES 4**   **PREP TIME: 5 MINUTES**

This energizing drink is a bit more tropical than it is Mediterranean, but it's still a celebration of Gaia (our beautiful earth), as well as nutrient dense, delicious, and extremely satisfying! It contains a generous portion of spinach, which provides an iron and vitamin A boost, as well as probiotic-rich yogurt and nutrient-dense, delicious fruits. For extra fun, you can freeze this into ice pops for an icy, nourishing summer treat. I prefer this with a slightly tart flavor, but if you'd like a little more sweetness, feel free to add a squeeze of agave nectar to the smoothie base.

1½ cups frozen mango chunks

1 frozen banana

1 cup frozen pineapple chunks

1 cup plain unsweetened nondairy yogurt

1 cup freshly squeezed orange juice, plus more as needed

Very large handful baby spinach

In a blender, combine the mango, banana, pineapple, yogurt, orange juice, and spinach. Blend until very smooth. If you're having trouble blending, add just a bit of extra juice or water and blend until smooth. Serve immediately.

Tasty Tip: This is one of my daughter's favorite smoothies, and she wants you to know it's also good with a few strawberries tossed in (although it won't be as green–green of a color if you do that). She'd also like to suggest you use coconut yogurt for the unsweetened nondairy yogurt, because it goes so well with the tropical fruits. However, there are some vegan Greek yogurts popping up in markets these days—feel free to experiment.

Per Serving: Calories: 128; Total Fat: 2g; Saturated Fat: 1g; Protein: 2g; Carbs: 30g; Fiber: 4g; Sodium: 38mg; Iron: 1mg

CHOCOLATE DREAM SMOOTHIE BOWL

GLUTEN-FREE, NUT-FREE, OIL-FREE, SOY-FREE   **SERVES 4**   **PREP TIME: 10 MINUTES**

I love a breakfast item that celebrates the pure joy of the Mediterranean philosophy. Food should be nutritious, but also scrumptious—and in this case, that means chocolate for breakfast every now and then. And why not? It's high in antioxidants (I mean, that's why we eat it, right?) and even contains serotonin, which can boost your mood. Have fun varying the toppings if you like—some other ideas are nuts, goji berries (or other dried fruits), and chia seeds.

6 very ripe frozen bananas

2½ cups unsweetened oat milk or any nondairy milk, plus more as needed

6 tablespoons cacao powder

1 tablespoon vanilla extract

¼ cup agave nectar or maple syrup (optional)

1 banana, sliced

2 cups sliced strawberries

1 cup granola (preferably plain, peanut butter, or chocolate)

¼ cup raw cacao nibs (optional)

1. In a blender or food processor, combine the frozen bananas, oat milk, cacao powder, vanilla, and agave (if using). Blend until very smooth. If too thick, add just enough additional oat milk to blend, being careful not to add too much or it will be too thin. (You're aiming for as thick as possible while still being able to blend it up.)

2. Divide the smoothie into 4 bowls and top each with banana and strawberry slices, ¼ cup granola, and 1 tablespoon cacao nibs (if using). Enjoy immediately.

Tasty Tip: For added lusciousness, why not add a scoop of peanut butter? You can blend it into the smoothie base or spoon it over the top. If doing that classic chocolate–peanut butter combination, some toppings that pair well are bananas, strawberries, chia seeds, cacao nibs, and peanuts or other nuts.

Per Serving: Calories: 416; Total Fat: 13g; Saturated Fat: 5g; Protein: 12g; Carbs: 82g; Fiber: 19g; Sodium: 236mg; Iron: 5mg

QUICK VANILLA CHIA PUDDING

GLUTEN-FREE, OIL-FREE, SOY-FREE   **SERVES 6**   **PREP TIME: 2 MINUTES, PLUS 3 HOURS FOR THICKENING**

If you're looking for a breakfast that's loaded with omega-3s, fiber, and antioxidants yet takes only 2 minutes of your time, this is it. I like to make a big batch because it lasts in the fridge for at least a week. Plus, it's great for anytime you need a healthy pick-me-up. Just a few bites of this energizing treat will keep you going between mealtimes. I love the consistency of this, but if you prefer a thicker pudding, simply increase the amount of chia seeds. Here's to powering your mornings with nutrient-dense deliciousness.

4 cups unsweetened plain or vanilla nondairy milk

²⁄₃ cup chia seeds

6 tablespoons pure maple syrup

1 ½ tablespoons vanilla extract

1 cup strawberries or raspberries

½ cup shelled pistachios or slivered almonds

1. In a large bowl, combine the milk, chia, maple syrup, and vanilla. Stir well, cover, and refrigerate for 3 to 4 hours, until thickened.

2. Stir again (sometimes the chia seeds like to stick together—they're friendly like that). Divide the pudding into 6 serving dishes and top with the berries and nuts.

Per Serving: Calories: 280; Total Fat: 15g; Saturated Fat: 1g; Protein: 7g; Carbs: 29g; Fiber: 11g; Sodium: 246mg; Iron: 4mg

SIMPLY DELICIOUS BANANA PANCAKES

NUT-FREE, SOY-FREE   SERVES 4   PREP TIME: 5 MINUTES / COOK TIME: 15 MINUTES

These simple, delicious, and extremely easy-to-make pancakes are on regular rotation in our home. The lazy chef in me likes them because it's easy to just mash up a banana in a large glass measuring cup and then add all the other ingredients to it. These fiber- and potassium-rich pancakes are great plain or drizzled with your favorite sweetener. However, for the full experience, top with a dollop of vegan Greek vanilla or plain yogurt, fresh banana slices, and maple syrup.

1 ripe banana

1 cup unsweetened nondairy milk

2 tablespoons olive, coconut, or sunflower oil, plus more for frying

1 cup whole-wheat pastry flour

½ teaspoon baking powder

¼ teaspoon baking soda

¼ teaspoon sea salt

1. In a bowl or large glass measuring cup, mash the peeled banana well with a fork. Add the nondairy milk and oil and stir well to combine. Add the flour, baking powder, baking soda, and salt. Stir just until thoroughly combined.

2. Heat a small amount of oil in a large skillet over medium heat. Once it's hot, pour in ¼ to ⅓ cup of the batter for each pancake, leaving about 2 inches between them. Don't make them too big or they'll be hard to flip.

3. Cook for 1 to 2 minutes until the bottoms are browned, then flip them. Once both sides are golden brown, transfer to a plate and serve.

Tasty Tip: For extra deliciousness, use vanilla-flavored nondairy milk or add vanilla extract to the batter (I use about 1 teaspoon). You can also add a dash of ground nutmeg or cinnamon if you want to spice things up.

Per Serving: Calories: 190; Total Fat: 9g; Saturated Fat: 1g; Protein: 3g; Carbs: 24g; Fiber: 4g; Sodium: 287mg; Iron: 1mg

LEAN, GREEN PROTEIN PANCAKES

GLUTEN-FREE, NUT-FREE, SOY-FREE   **SERVES 4**
PREP TIME: 10 MINUTES, PLUS OVERNIGHT SOAKING / COOK TIME: 10 MINUTES

Although these pancakes aren't a traditional Mediterranean dish, they follow the dietary principles beautifully. And don't let the name fool you—yes, these are lean and green, but they're also delicious (especially when paired with tahini dressing, as suggested in the serving tip). I absolutely love starting my day with a plate of these hearty pancakes, because they're so satisfying, yet very light and nutrient dense. You can feel like a superstar when you opt for this fiber-rich, protein-packed, ultra-nutritious breakfast!

1 cup dried red lentils, soaked in water for at least 8 hours

¾ cup water

2 tablespoons freshly squeezed lemon juice

3 garlic cloves, peeled

1 teaspoon sea salt

1 cup stemmed and finely chopped kale or spinach

8 to 10 Kalamata olives, pitted and chopped

Oil, for frying (optional)

1. Drain the lentils, rinse with fresh water, and drain well again.

2. In a blender, combine the lentils, water, lemon juice, garlic, and salt. Blend until very smooth. Remove and stir in the kale and olives.

3. In a large nonstick skillet, heat a small amount of oil (if using) over medium-high heat. Pour in the batter to make 3-inch pancakes. Cook the pancakes for 2 to 3 minutes until dry around the edges and golden brown on the underside, then flip them. When golden brown on both sides, transfer to a plate. Serve warm.

Serving Tip: I often eat these plain on-the-go, but they're definitely more delicious when drizzled with Easy Tahini-Herb Dressing (page 26).

Per Serving: Calories: 196; Total Fat: 2g; Saturated Fat: 0g; Protein: 13g; Carbs: 32g; Fiber: 15g; Sodium: 578mg; Iron: 4mg

TOFU-KALE SCRAMBLE

GLUTEN-FREE, NUT-FREE   **SERVES 4**   **PREP TIME: 5 MINUTES / COOK TIME: 10 MINUTES**

Here's a Mediterranean take on the classic tofu scramble, which I've been making (and eating in restaurants) for decades. This twist is fun because it calls for even more garlic and brightly colored vegetables, which give it a beta-carotene boost. Let's also not forget the Kalamata olives, which lend such a flavor kick to any party they attend. Be sure to use actual Kalamata olives, not regular black olives, for the best flavor. Serve this scramble alongside Lemony Potatoes (page 38) and Hemera's Strawberry Smoothie (page 51) or Green Gaia Smoothie (page 52) for a glorious, nourishing breakfast. For additional yumminess, add some fresh herbs to the final result—dill, oregano, and rosemary work nicely here.

2 tablespoons extra-virgin olive oil

1 (14-ounce) package firm or extra-firm tofu

2 tablespoons nutritional yeast

½ teaspoon ground turmeric

2 cups firmly packed stemmed and thinly sliced kale

½ cup grated carrot

6 garlic cloves, minced or pressed

½ teaspoon sea salt

10 Kalamata olives, pitted and chopped

2 teaspoons freshly squeezed lemon juice

Freshly ground black pepper (optional)

1. In a large skillet, heat the olive oil over medium-high heat. Using your hands, squeeze the excess moisture from the tofu over the sink, then crumble it into the pan. Add the nutritional yeast and turmeric. Stir well to combine and cook for 2 minutes.

2. Add the kale and sauté for 3 minutes, stirring often.

3. Add the carrot, garlic, and salt and cook for about 5 minutes, stirring often, until the tofu is golden brown and the kale is nicely wilted. Add the olives and lemon juice, stir well, and cook for about 30 seconds until just heated through. Remove the skillet from the heat and serve. If desired, sprinkle with additional salt and pepper.

Ingredient Tip: Nutritional yeast is a vegan staple that's absolutely indispensable when it comes to making a good tofu scramble. You can find it in any health food store and often in the bulk section as well. It has a mild, nutty, cheesy flavor and is very high in B vitamins and iron.

Per Serving: Calories: 223; Total Fat: 15g; Saturated Fat: 2g; Protein: 15g; Carbs: 13g; Fiber: 4g; Sodium: 366mg; Iron: 3mg

MEDITERRANEAN AVOCADO TOAST

OIL-FREE, SOY-FREE   **SERVES 4**   **PREP TIME: 5 MINUTES / COOK TIME: 5 MINUTES**

Avocado toast is basically everywhere—like, *everywhere*. I mean, how could you not like a dish that combines two of the world's best things: avocado and carbs? Avocado, for its rich, creamy amazingness, as well as its monounsaturated fatty acids and the fact that it has more potassium than a banana—and carbs because they're, well, *carbs*. And don't let the Aleppo pepper scare you away—you can omit it if you prefer less heat (or don't have it on hand), or substitute another hot pepper, as suggested in the ingredient tip below.

¼ cup pine nuts

2 avocados, peeled and pitted

2 tablespoons freshly squeezed lemon juice

½ teaspoon sea salt

4 whole-grain or sourdough bread slices

1 tablespoon nutritional yeast

½ teaspoon Aleppo pepper

1. In a large dry skillet, toast the pine nuts over medium-low heat, stirring often, for 2 to 3 minutes until lightly browned and aromatic. Transfer them to a plate immediately and set aside.

2. In a small bowl, combine the avocados, lemon juice, and salt and mash together well.

3. In a toaster or broiler, toast the bread and spread each piece with one-quarter of the avocado mixture. Top evenly with the pine nuts and finish with a sprinkling of nutritional yeast and Aleppo pepper. Serve immediately.

Ingredient Tip: Aleppo peppers, which hail from Turkey, have a mild heat and a slightly fruity flavor. You can find them at specialty stores and some major supermarkets. You can also simply substitute red pepper flakes or pink peppercorns if need be.

Per Serving: Calories: 304; Total Fat: 21g; Saturated Fat: 3g; Protein: 9g; Carbs: 25g; Fiber: 10g; Sodium: 378mg; Iron: 2mg

BREAKFAST FARRO

OIL-FREE, SOY-FREE   SERVES 3 TO 4   PREP TIME: 5 MINUTES / COOK TIME: 30 MINUTES

Farro is considered an ancient grain—it was one of the first cereal grains to be cultivated in what is now the Middle East, and it remains relatively unchanged today. Farro has a wonderfully chewy texture that will pleasantly surprise you if you've never tried it. It's a good source of fiber, protein, niacin, magnesium, and zinc and works well in both sweet and savory dishes. If you're an oatmeal person, I encourage you to try this version of hot cereal: it's chewy and filling, and doesn't need any sweeteners beyond the dried fruit.

1 cup farro

1 cup water

1 cup unsweetened plain or vanilla almond milk

2 teaspoons vanilla extract

1 teaspoon ground cinnamon

⅛ teaspoon freshly ground nutmeg

2 Medjool dates, pitted and chopped

4 dried apricots, chopped

3 tablespoons chopped pistachios

1. In a medium saucepan, toast the farro for 2 to 3 minutes over medium heat. Add the water, almond milk, vanilla, cinnamon, and nutmeg. Bring the mixture to a boil, then reduce the heat to low and simmer, partially covered, for 20 minutes.

2. Remove the lid, stir in the dates and apricots, and cook for another 5 minutes until most of the liquid is absorbed and the farro is soft but still chewy. Spoon into bowls and sprinkle with the pistachios.

Per Serving: Calories: 330; Total Fat: 5g; Saturated Fat: 0g; Protein: 8g; Carbs: 62g; Fiber: 10g; Sodium: 141mg; Iron: 3mg

SAVORY GREEK BREAKFAST, TWO WAYS

NUT-FREE, SOY-FREE   SERVES 4 TO 6   PREP TIME: VARIABLE / COOK TIME: VARIABLE

A lot of us think sweet when we think of breakfast, but, in the Mediterranean, breakfast often consists of various savory items on a plate. Imagine you're in Greece, sitting by the water, slowly savoring a variety of goodies on your plate. What better way to start the day? This is less of a recipe and more of a brunch menu, but I highly recommend trying it. The concept revolves around having a few delicious savory items, a dip, some bread, and a calm, focused attitude to start the day. And in case you haven't guessed, this is a fantastic way to use up leftovers, so feel free to make extras of your favorite savory Mediterranean dishes and use them up this way.

Suggested items

Classic Baba Ghanoush (page 22)

Happy Hummus (page 23)

Lemony Potatoes (page 38)

Garlicky Mushrooms (page 36)

Ful Medames (page 31)

For the plate

4 Pita Bread (page 65) rounds, store-bought pita bread, or sourdough bread slices

For the wrap

Whole-grain tortillas

To make a savory breakfast plate

Place your desired items on a plate and serve with warm bread for dipping and scooping. Aim for at least one dip, one vegetable, and one bean dish.

To make a savory breakfast wrap

Warm whole-grain tortillas in a skillet over medium heat, then transfer to a plate. Top with the items of your choice, roll up, and enjoy!

RAINBOW WRAPS, P. 70

5

BREADS, WRAPS, AND SANDWICHES

ZA'ATAR CRISPS

NUT-FREE, SOY-FREE   **SERVES 4**   **PREP TIME: 2 MINUTES / COOK TIME: 10 MINUTES**

These tasty crisps couldn't be easier to make. There's nothing like za'atar to give a delicious, tangy spin to almost anything, so it's definitely worth keeping on hand. Serve these yummy little crunchers as a scoop for Happy Hummus (page 23), Classic Baba Ghanoush (page 22), or Tangy Cheese Dip (page 25). They also make a great way to start the day combined with a serving of Tofu-Kale Scramble (page 57).

4 teaspoons olive oil, plus more for greasing, divided

2 (8-inch) whole-grain tortillas

3 tablespoons za'atar

1. Preheat the oven to 400°F. Lightly grease a rimmed baking sheet with olive oil.

2. Stack the tortillas and cut them into 8 wedges, for a total of 16 pieces. Place the pieces in a single layer on the baking sheet. Brush the tops with 2 teaspoons of olive oil. Sprinkle the za'atar evenly over the pieces (if it seems like too much, it's just about right). Drizzle the tops with the remaining 2 teaspoons of olive oil.

3. Bake for 5 to 10 minutes until lightly browned and crisp. Serve warm and enjoy.

Ingredient Tip: With origins in the Levant region (the Eastern Mediterranean), za'atar is a tangy and delightful combination of sumac, thyme, and other spices. It can be found in health food stores, international markets, or online. It's great in Fattoush Salad (page 78) or sprinkled over Happy Hummus (page 23) or Classic Baba Ghanoush (page 22).

Simple Swap: If you're gluten free, brown rice tortillas are a delicious and healthy swap for the whole-grain tortillas. Please note that they may cook more quickly than other tortillas, so keep an eye on them while they bake.

Per Serving: Calories: 110; Total Fat: 7g; Saturated Fat: 1g; Protein: 3g; Carbs: 12g; Fiber: 3g; Sodium: 230mg; Iron: 1mg

PITA BREAD

NUT-FREE, SOY-FREE   SERVES 8

PREP TIME: 15 MINUTES, PLUS 1½ HOURS FOR RISING / COOK TIME: 30 MINUTES

Pita is a delicious and versatile bread that's been enjoyed for centuries in the Eastern Mediterranean and beyond. It is also easy to make, cooks quickly, and reheats well. You can use this bread as a pocket to hold Falafel (page 44) and Easy Tahini-Herb Dressing (page 26), as a companion to Fattoush Salad (page 78), or as a way to scoop up Classic Baba Ghanoush (page 22), Happy Hummus (page 23), or Vibrant Beet Hummus (page 24). If the pita is made ahead of time or if you have leftovers, it can be heated right on a gas burner for about 10 seconds on each side. Heating makes the pita more pliable and brings back that just-baked flavor.

2 cups all-purpose flour, plus more for dusting

1 cup whole-wheat flour

1 tablespoon instant yeast

2 teaspoons sugar or agave nectar

1 teaspoon sea salt

1¼ cups very warm water (90°F to 100°F), plus more as needed

1 tablespoon extra-virgin olive oil, plus more for greasing

1. In a medium bowl, combine the flours, yeast, sugar, and salt. Stir in the water and olive oil until a shaggy dough forms. Turn out the dough onto a clean, lightly floured work surface and knead for 5 minutes, or until smooth and pliable. The dough should be tacky but not sticky, similar to pizza dough. Add more flour or water as needed to achieve the right texture.

2. Form the dough into a ball. Drizzle a little olive oil into a clean mixing bowl and put the dough in, turning it over once to coat the ball with the oil. Cover the bowl with a clean dish towel or plastic wrap and let rise in a warm place until roughly double in size, about 1½ hours.

Continued on next page

3. Turn out the dough onto a lightly floured work surface and cut it into 8 equal pieces. Keep the pieces covered until ready to use.

4. Heat a nonstick or cast iron skillet over medium heat. Brush lightly with oil. Using a rolling pin, roll a piece of dough into a round about 6 inches in diameter. Place it in the pan and cook for 2 minutes until browned in places. Use tongs to flip it and cook for 2 to 3 minutes more. Repeat with the remaining pieces.

Tasty Tip: Homemade pita bread makes a great base for Za'atar Crisps (page 64). Or, whip up some garlic crisps by brushing the prepared pita bread with olive oil, topping with chopped garlic (and plenty of it), and baking at 400°F until browned and crisp.

Ingredient Tip: Make sure to use instant yeast, which can be combined directly with dry ingredients. If you prefer to use active yeast instead, follow this extra step: Put the warm water in the mixing bowl, sprinkle with the yeast, and stir in the sugar and 1 cup of all-purpose flour. Let it sit for 15 minutes or until the mixture begins to bubble. Then you can stir in the remaining ingredients and continue as instructed.

Per Serving: Calories: 177; Total Fat: 3g; Saturated Fat: 0g; Protein: 5g; Carbs: 33g; Fiber: 3g; Sodium: 235mg; Iron: 2mg

EASY CHICKPEA FLATBREADS

GLUTEN-FREE, NUT-FREE, OIL-FREE, SOY-FREE   **MAKES ABOUT 12 FLATBREADS**
PREP TIME: 5 MINUTES / COOK TIME: 10 MINUTES

These flatbreads come together in just a few minutes and are great alongside salads or for scooping up dips like Classic Baba Ghanoush (page 22), Vibrant Beet Hummus (page 24), or Tangy Cheese Dip (page 25). You can also make a delicious, high-protein wrap by filling a flatbread with Garlicky Mushrooms (page 36), Happy Hummus (page 23), and Quinoa Tabbouleh (page 80). If you have a good nonstick skillet, you can keep these oil free, but you can also add a little olive oil to the pan if desired.

For the dry mix

1½ cups chickpea flour

1½ teaspoons nutritional yeast

1 teaspoon onion granules or onion powder

¾ teaspoon sea salt

⅜ teaspoon baking soda

For the batter

3 cups water

¼ cup freshly squeezed lemon juice

To make the dry mix

> In a jar with a tight-fitting lid, combine the flour, nutritional yeast, onion granules, salt, and baking soda. Close the jar and shake well to combine thoroughly.

To make the batter

1. In a bowl, whisk together the dry mix, water, and lemon juice.

2. Heat a large nonstick skillet over medium-high heat. Once hot, pour ¼ cup of the batter into the center of the pan. Using the back of a soup spoon, immediately swirl the batter out in a circular motion so that your flatbread is round(ish), thin, and uniform in thickness.

Continued on next page

3. Once the flatbread has bubbles on top and looks dry around the edges, flip it. Cook until the other side is golden brown. This should be a fairly quick process, about 1 minute per side. Transfer to a plate.

4. Repeat until the batter is used up. Store leftover flatbreads in an airtight container in the refrigerator for up to 3 days.

Technique Tip: These take a little practice to form into round flatbreads in the pan, but I say "round(ish)" in the instructions for a reason—there's no need to get all perfectionist with these things. As long as they're (relatively) flat and not too thick, they'll be fine. If your batter becomes too thick at any point, whisk in a smidge more water.

Love Your Leftovers: To make just 2 flatbreads at a time, use ¼ cup of the dry mix, ¼ cup water, and 1 teaspoon lemon juice. Store the remaining dry mix in a cool, dry place or in the refrigerator for up to 1 month or in the freezer for up to 6 months.

Per Serving: Calories: 53; Total Fat: 1g; Saturated Fat: 0g; Protein: 4g; Carbs: 8g; Fiber: 2g; Sodium: 178mg; Iron: 1mg

EGGPLANT LOVER'S WRAPS

NUT-FREE, SOY-FREE　　　**SERVES 6**　　　**PREP TIME: 10 MINUTES / COOK TIME: 20 MINUTES**

If you're at all like me (unreasonably obsessed with eggplant anything), you want to get as much of this amazing vegetable into your meals as possible. So, of course, I had to come up with a way to sneak two forms of eggplant into one dish. Here we pair creamy, rich baba ghanoush with gooey eggplant slices (and some other non-eggplant things to maintain an air of respectability) to form one yummy, nutrient-dense wrap. Eggplant lovers, unite.

1 (8-ounce) eggplant, cut into ¼-inch thick rounds

3 tablespoons olive oil

1 teaspoon garlic granules or 6 garlic cloves, minced or pressed

Sea salt, as desired

6 Pita Bread (page 65) rounds, store-bought pita bread, or whole-grain tortillas

1 recipe Classic Baba Ghanoush (page 22)

¾ cup sliced roasted red peppers

¾ cup thinly sliced red onion

1½ cups arugula or baby spinach

¾ cup sliced dill pickles or banana peppers (optional)

1. Preheat the oven to 400°F.

2. Place the eggplant rounds in a single layer on a rimmed baking sheet. Drizzle the olive oil evenly on top of the eggplant and sprinkle with the garlic. Season with salt and turn each piece over to coat thoroughly in the oil.

3. Bake for 10 to 15 minutes, until the undersides are nicely browned. Flip the slices and bake for another 5 to 10 minutes until the eggplant slices are very tender and golden brown.

4. To assemble the wraps, spread each pita bread round with baba ghanoush. Add the eggplant slices, red peppers, onion, arugula, and pickles (if using). Wrap up and enjoy!

Simple Swap: If you're gluten free, brown rice tortillas are a delicious and healthy swap for the pita bread.

Per Serving: Calories: 411; Total Fat: 22g; Saturated Fat: 3g; Protein: 9g; Carbs: 47g; Fiber: 12g; Sodium: 528mg; Iron: 2mg

RAINBOW WRAPS

GLUTEN-FREE, NUT-FREE, SOY-FREE   **SERVES 4**   **PREP TIME: 15 MINUTES**

Here's my take on one of my all-time favorite sandwiches: the "Hippie Chick" from Nature's Oasis in Durango, Colorado. This wrap makes me feel like I'm eating the rainbow (hello, every nutrient under the sun). The secret to making the flavor really pop is to add banana peppers. This version also uses iron-rich, energy-boosting collard leaves rather than bread. The trick to making a collard leaf wrap well is to trim the stem a bit before you roll it up. However, if you prefer, omit the collard and just serve the toppings on whole-grain bread instead.

4 large collard green leaves

1 recipe Happy Hummus (page 23) or Vibrant Beet Hummus (page 24)

1 avocado, peeled, pitted, and sliced or chopped

1 cup finely chopped red cabbage

1 cup grated carrot

1 cup thinly sliced cucumber

⅓ cup sliced peperoncini or banana peppers

1. Place a collard leaf stem-side up on a plate. Using a sharp knife, slice off most of the stem, so that it's flush with the leaf. If you accidentally cut into the leaf, don't worry—you can roll that part up. What you're aiming for is a "tortilla" leaf, so that you've got an even, flat surface and no thick stem sticking up.

2. With the stem-side facing you, spread the middle of the leaf with one-quarter of the hummus, top with one-quarter of the avocado, and finish with one-quarter each of the cabbage, carrot, cucumber, and peperoncini. Roll the bottom of the collard leaf up and over the fillings. Roll the sides in toward the center so that they're parallel to each other. Then, roll up the wrap all the way to form a green "burrito."

3. Repeat with the remaining collard leaves and fillings. Serve immediately or store in an airtight container in the refrigerator for up to 2 days.

Love Your Leftovers: You'll likely have some collard leaves leftover, and that's a great problem to have. You can juice them and add them to green smoothies or sauté them in a little olive oil with garlic and lemon juice for a delicious, iron-rich side dish.

Per Serving: Calories: 312; Total Fat: 22g; Saturated Fat: 2g; Protein: 16g; Carbs: 52g; Fiber: 18g; Sodium: 320mg; Iron: 6mg

APHRODITE'S OLIVE SANDWICH

SOY-FREE   SERVES 4   PREP TIME: 10 MINUTES

Aphrodite is the Greek goddess of love and pleasure, which is pretty appropriate for this sandwich. Yes, it's simple, but the combination of ingredients tastes wonderfully complex, rich, and satisfying. In Greek mythology, Aphrodite wore a belt that had the power to make people fall in love with whoever was wearing it. Basically, this sandwich is your belt.

8 sourdough bread slices

1 recipe Macadamia-Rosemary Cheese (page 27)

16 Kalamata olives, pitted and sliced

2 tomatoes, sliced

⅓ cup chopped fresh basil

¼ cup thinly sliced red onion

Place 4 bread slices on plates. Spread a thick layer of the cheese on each slice, then top with the olives, tomatoes, basil, and onion. Cover the sandwiches with the remaining 4 bread slices, cut, and serve.

Tasty Tip: To further increase the love factor here, substitute sun-dried tomatoes for half of the fresh tomatoes, and sneak in a few marinated artichoke hearts!

Simple Swap: If you want added health benefits and fiber, go for a whole-grain or sprouted bread. If you like, toast the bread for a little added crunch.

Per Serving: Calories: 536; Total Fat: 36g; Saturated Fat: 6g; Protein: 15g; Carbs: 49g; Fiber: 9g; Sodium: 540mg; Iron: 5mg

TABBOULEH LETTUCE WRAPS

GLUTEN-FREE, NUT-FREE, SOY-FREE   SERVES 8   PREP TIME: 15 MINUTES

I love using lettuce leaves instead of tortillas or bread, as they add lots of nutrients (chlorophyll, iron, and potassium) and a great crunch. And you're going to adore the combination of tastes and textures here—creamy hummus is the perfect base for the lemony tabbouleh, and the olives and tomatoes lend additional color, texture, and complementary flavors.

---

1 recipe Happy Hummus (page 23)

16 large romaine lettuce leaves

1 recipe Quinoa Tabbouleh (page 80)

1½ cups cherry tomatoes, halved

32 Kalamata olives, pitted and chopped

Spread a little hummus down the center of each lettuce leaf, then add a spoonful of tabbouleh. Top evenly with tomatoes and olives. Serve two on each plate.

Simple Swap: Vibrant Beet Hummus (page 24) or Classic Baba Ghanoush (page 22) can be used instead of Happy Hummus to change up the flavor a bit. Additionally, you can substitute red or green leaf lettuce for the romaine. These varieties will simply need to be wrapped around the fillings a bit more, as they're larger and more foldable than romaine.

Per Serving: Calories: 324; Total Fat: 19g; Saturated Fat: 2g; Protein: 11g; Carbs: 33g; Fiber: 8g; Sodium: 477mg; Iron: 5mg

HARISSA TOFU AND ROASTED VEGETABLE SANDWICH

SERVES 6   **PREP TIME: 25 MINUTES / COOK TIME: 20 MINUTES**

I like to serve this delicious, satisfying sandwich alongside Catalonian Kale Salad (page 85) for a nourishing meal. If you want to make these in a pinch during the week, simply keep the Harissa Tofu (page 30), Tangy Cheese Dip (page 25), and some roasted vegetables on hand in the fridge. That way they'll be ready to go in a literal minute. For an extra flavor boost, add some roasted garlic. No matter how you slice it, this is one yummy sandwich.

Olive oil cooking spray

1 onion, thinly sliced

2 zucchini, thinly sliced

Sea salt

12 whole-grain bread slices

1 recipe Tangy Cheese Dip (page 25)

1 recipe Harissa Tofu (page 30)

½ cup sliced peperoncini or banana peppers

1. Preheat the oven to 400°F. Spray a large rimmed baking sheet with cooking spray.

2. Scatter the onion and zucchini slices on the prepared sheet. Spray the tops with cooking spray and sprinkle with salt. Roast for 10 minutes, stir, and continue roasting until tender and nicely browned, about 10 minutes more. Remove and set aside.

3. To assemble, spread 6 slices of bread generously with the cheese. Top evenly with the tofu and roasted vegetables. Add the peperoncini, top with the remaining bread, and dig in.

Simple Swap: You can vary this recipe by using other vegetables instead of (or in addition to) the onion and zucchini. Some that work well include roasted red peppers, artichoke hearts, Kalamata olives, eggplant, and yellow summer squash. If you omit the roasted onion, you can add a little thinly sliced red onion (raw) for that oniony kick.

Per Serving: Calories: 482; Total Fat: 17g; Saturated Fat: 2g; Protein: 28g; Carbs: 59g; Fiber: 12g; Sodium: 583mg; Iron: 6mg

FALAFEL WRAPS

NUT-FREE, SOY-FREE   SERVES 4   PREP TIME: 15 MINUTES / COOK TIME: 45 MINUTES

There's just something about falafel wraps that's so satisfying—the crisp and spice of the falafel, the creamy tahini dressing, and the crunchy fresh vegetables. I'm personally pro-pickle as well—my long-held belief is that dill pickles add the perfect tang to a falafel wrap and should always be included. Even if you disagree and decide to omit the pickles, this wrap will make you (almost as) happy.

4 Pita Bread (page 65) rounds, store-bought pita bread, or whole-grain tortillas

1 recipe Falafel (page 44)

4 lettuce leaves, preferably red leaf or romaine, chopped

2 tomatoes, chopped

½ small red onion, minced

4 dill pickles, chopped or sliced

1 recipe Easy Tahini-Herb Dressing (page 26)

On a warm burner or in a dry skillet, toast the pita rounds until warm, about 1 minute. Fill each with 4 or 5 falafel, then add the lettuce, tomatoes, onion, and pickles. Add a generous drizzle of tahini dressing over the fillings. Serve immediately.

Simple Swap: You can use whole-grain tortillas (or brown rice tortillas, if you're gluten free) instead of the pita rounds if you prefer. Simply warm them in the same manner as the pita bread, one tortilla at a time, then roll them up when filled.

Per Serving: Calories: 750; Total Fat: 42g; Saturated Fat: 6g; Protein: 24g; Carbs: 76g; Fiber: 13g; Sodium: 2214mg; Iron: 13mg

EGGPLANT "GYROS"

NUT-FREE, SOY-FREE   SERVES 6   PREP TIME: 15 MINUTES / COOK TIME: 30 MINUTES

Gyros are a staple in Greece, and this whole-food version uses high-fiber, nutrient-dense eggplant. One of my absolute favorite vegetables, savory eggplant has a host of nutritional benefits, including vitamins C and K, fiber, thiamin, and niacin. Drizzled with iron-rich tahini dressing, this is a handheld meal that's delicious *and* good for you.

¼ cup olive oil, plus more for greasing

2 medium eggplants, stemmed and cut lengthwise into 8 (½-inch-thick) slices

1½ teaspoons sea salt

1 tablespoon garlic granules or powder

1 tablespoon dried oregano

2 teaspoons dried thyme

2 teaspoons ground cumin

1 teaspoon freshly ground black pepper

6 Pita Bread (page 65) rounds, store-bought pita bread, or whole-grain tortillas

½ red onion, thinly sliced

2 tomatoes, chopped or sliced

1 recipe Easy Tahini-Herb Dressing (page 26)

1. Preheat the oven to 400°F. Lightly grease two rimmed baking sheets with olive oil.

2. Place the eggplant slices in a single layer on the prepared baking sheets. Brush the tops with the olive oil, then sprinkle with the salt, garlic, oregano, thyme, cumin, and pepper. Bake for 10 minutes, flip each slice, and continue baking for another 10 to 15 minutes, until the eggplant is very soft and nicely browned.

3. In a skillet, warm the pita rounds over medium-high heat for about 1 minute until warmed through. Fill each with eggplant, onion slices, and tomatoes, then drizzle generously with the tahini dressing. Serve immediately.

Per Serving: Calories: 560; Total Fat: 33g; Saturated Fat: 5g; Protein: 15g; Carbs: 60g; Fiber: 16g; Sodium: 670mg; Iron: 5mg

FALAFEL SALAD, P. 86

SALADS AND SOUPS

FATTOUSH SALAD

NUT-FREE, SOY-FREE   SERVES 4   PREP TIME: 10 MINUTES / COOK TIME: 10 MINUTES

There's something so satisfying about a good fattoush salad. It basically has everything: crispy bread, crunchy vegetables, and the bright tang of lemon and mint. I like to eat this alongside some Happy Hummus (page 23) and Delicious Dolmas (page 34) for a fully satisfying yet light meal.

4 tablespoons olive oil, divided, plus more for greasing

4 Pita Bread (page 65) rounds or store-bought pita bread, cut into 1½-inch pieces

1 pound cherry tomatoes, halved

2 cups diced cucumber

½ cup thinly sliced fresh mint

¼ cup chopped scallions, both white and green parts

Juice of 1 lemon

1 tablespoon za'atar

½ teaspoon sea salt

Freshly ground black pepper

1. Preheat the oven to 400°F. Lightly grease a rimmed baking sheet with olive oil.

2. Arrange the pita pieces in a single layer on the prepared baking sheet. Brush the tops with 1 tablespoon of olive oil. Bake for 5 to 10 minutes until golden brown and crisp. Set aside.

3. In a large bowl, mix the tomatoes, cucumber, mint, scallions, remaining 3 tablespoons of olive oil, lemon juice, za'atar, salt, and pepper. Stir well to combine.

4. Add the pita crisps and gently toss until they're thoroughly coated with the vegetable mixture. Let sit for about 5 minutes until the pita has absorbed some of the marinade but is still crisp. Stir once more and serve.

Ingredient Tip: You can omit the za'atar if you don't have it on hand, although it does add a lovely, unique flavor to this dish. If you're not using it, add a little more salt and pepper, and some oregano or basil to taste.

Simple Swap: You may substitute whole-grain tortillas for the pita bread, or brown rice tortillas for a gluten-free salad. Gluten-free tortillas tend to cook faster than pita rounds, so keep an eye on them and remove as soon as they begin to brown.

Per Serving: Calories: 323; Total Fat: 15g; Saturated Fat: 2g; Protein: 7g; Carbs: 41g; Fiber: 4g; Sodium: 569mg; Iron: 3mg

THE VEGAN GREEK

GLUTEN-FREE, NUT-FREE   **SERVES 6**   **PREP TIME: 15 MINUTES**

Who says eschewing animal products means you can't enjoy a gorgeous Greek salad? Not me! This recipe uses tofu instead of feta for a simple plant-based swap. There's so much flavor in the dressing, olives, and crunchy vegetables that the only complaints you'll get are from people who want leftovers after the last bit of salad is eaten up. Serve this alongside Happy Hummus (page 23) or Classic Baba Ghanoush (page 22) and Za'atar Crisps (page 64) for a sublimely satisfying and nourishing meal.

For the dressing

½ cup olive oil

⅓ cup apple cider vinegar

4 garlic cloves, minced or pressed

1 teaspoon dried basil

1 teaspoon dried oregano

Sea salt

Freshly ground black pepper

For the salad

8 ounces firm tofu

8 cups chopped romaine lettuce

½ cup thinly sliced red onion

1½ cups chopped tomato

1½ cups thinly sliced cucumber

18 Kalamata olives, pitted and sliced

To make the dressing

In a small bowl, whisk together the olive oil, vinegar, garlic, basil, oregano, salt, and pepper.

To make the salad

1. Using your hands, squeeze the excess water from the tofu over the sink, then crumble it into a bowl. Stir the dressing well and drizzle about ¼ cup over the tofu. Toss to coat.

2. Divide the lettuce among serving bowls and top with the seasoned tofu. Add the onion, tomato, cucumber, and olives. Drizzle with dressing to taste and serve.

Love Your Leftovers: If you end up with leftover dressing, it will keep for several weeks in the fridge. It's delicious on most salads, as well as a great way to liven up grilled vegetables and baked potatoes.

Per Serving: Calories: 229; Total Fat: 20g; Saturated Fat: 3g; Protein: 5g; Carbs: 10g; Fiber: 3g; Sodium: 168mg; Iron: 4mg

QUINOA TABBOULEH

GLUTEN-FREE, NUT-FREE, SOY-FREE   **SERVES 4**   **PREP TIME: 10 MINUTES / COOK TIME: 20 MINUTES**

This is a gluten-free twist on a Greek staple, bulgur tabbouleh. Quinoa works just as well here, and is extremely high in calcium, protein, and iron. There's also some major detoxifying and immune-boosting action going on thanks to the chlorophyll-rich parsley. I love the lemony bright-ness of a full-flavored tabbouleh, and this recipe delivers just that. It has ended up being one of my go-to travel staples because it makes delicious leftovers that last for days.

¾ cup quinoa, rinsed and drained

1½ cups water

¾ cup diced cucumber

3 cups minced fresh curly parsley

¼ cup minced fresh mint

½ cup minced onion

6 tablespoons freshly squeezed lemon juice

2 tablespoons extra-virgin olive oil

¾ teaspoon sea salt

1. In a small pot, combine the quinoa and water and bring to a boil over medium-high heat. Reduce the heat to low, cover the pot, and simmer for 15 to 20 minutes until all of the water has been absorbed. Remove the quinoa from the heat, uncover, and fluff with a fork. Set aside for a few minutes to cool slightly, fluffing with a fork occasionally to release steam.

2. Stir in the cucumber, parsley, mint, onion, lemon juice, olive oil, and salt. Mix well and serve warm or cold. Store leftovers in an airtight container in the refrigerator for up to 5 days.

Per Serving: Calories: 211; Total Fat: 10g; Saturated Fat: 2g; Protein: 7g; Carbs: 26g; Fiber: 4g; Sodium: 390mg; Iron: 5mg

AVOCADO-CITRUS SALAD

GLUTEN-FREE   SERVES 4   PREP TIME: 10 MINUTES

The creaminess of avocado and bright tangy freshness of orange and grapefruit are a match made in heaven. These vibrant fruits also make a pretty dish—feel free to put it together in a fun, artistic way! This satisfying salad is high in fiber, omega-3s, vitamin C, and antioxidants. Plus, it's an excellent source of potassium, which helps your body release sodium. To make this a complete meal, serve over a bed of quinoa or couscous—perhaps with some Ful Medames (page 31) or Harissa Tofu (page 30) on the side.

For the dressing

¼ cup freshly squeezed lime juice

¼ cup freshly squeezed orange juice

3 tablespoons coconut sugar or agave nectar

2 tablespoons extra-virgin olive oil

2 teaspoons tamari, shoyu, or soy sauce

1 teaspoon sea salt

For the salad

1 large red grapefruit, peeled and sliced

1 medium orange, peeled and sliced

4 cups chopped romaine or red leaf lettuce

2 avocados, peeled, pitted, and chopped or sliced

½ cup pistachios, shelled and chopped

To make the dressing

In a small bowl, whisk together the lime juice, orange juice, coconut sugar, olive oil, tamari, and salt. Note that the coconut sugar may take a few minutes to fully dissolve.

To make the salad

1. If the grapefruit or orange slices have any white portions (pith) around the edges, gently peel or cut them off, as they lend a bitter flavor.

2. Divide the lettuce among serving plates. Top with the avocado, grapefruit, and orange. Drizzle with the dressing and sprinkle with pistachios right before serving.

Tasty Tip: Add pomegranate seeds for extra sweet crunch and an even prettier plate!

Simple Swap: You can use just orange or grapefruit if you have only one on hand, but if you choose to omit the grapefruit, you'll want to reduce the coconut sugar by about 1 tablespoon in the dressing as you won't have grapefruit's tartness to offset the sweetness. Baby spinach also works well as the base for this salad.

Per Serving: Calories: 364; Total Fat: 24g; Saturated Fat: 3g; Protein: 5g; Carbs: 40g; Fiber: 9g; Sodium: 667mg; Iron: 1mg

FRENCH LENTIL SALAD

NUT-FREE, SOY-FREE   SERVES 4   PREP TIME: 15 MINUTES / COOK TIME: 45 MINUTES

This hearty salad is both casual enough for an everyday meal and special (and pretty) enough to serve at parties. French (Puy) lentils are grown in the Puy region of central France, and because of the volcanic soil they're grown in, they have a somewhat peppery flavor. French lentils are a bit firmer than brown lentils, but they have such an appealing texture and taste. However, if you don't love them, you can substitute brown or green lentils.

1 cup dried French (Puy) lentils

2¼ cups water

2 teaspoons dried rosemary

2 tablespoons extra-virgin olive oil

4 cups crusty artisan, whole-grain, or gluten-free bread cubes (about 1-inch cubes)

¼ teaspoon sea salt

4 cups baby greens (spinach, arugula, and/or baby kale)

1 medium carrot, diced or grated

½ cup thinly sliced red onion

1 recipe Luscious Moroccan Sauce (page 29)

¼ cup pomegranate seeds

1. In large pot, combine the lentils, water, and rosemary and bring to a boil over high heat. Reduce the heat to low and simmer until the water is absorbed and the lentils are tender yet still a bit firm, about 45 minutes.

2. Meanwhile, in a large skillet, heat the olive oil over medium-high heat and add the bread cubes. Sprinkle with salt and stir well. Cook for 5 to 10 minutes, stirring often, until golden brown. Remove from the heat and set aside.

3. When the lentils are ready, divide the greens among serving bowls and top evenly with the lentils. Add the carrot and onion on top of the lentils and drizzle with the desired amount of sauce. Top with the croutons and pomegranate seeds and serve immediately.

Per Serving: Calories: 611; Total Fat: 9g; Saturated Fat: 1g; Protein: 16g; Carbs: 116g; Fiber: 17g; Sodium: 522mg; Iron: 6mg

BROCCOLI, WALNUT, AND FIG SALAD

GLUTEN-FREE, SOY-FREE **SERVES 4** **PREP TIME: 10 MINUTES**

This simple salad celebrates the fabulousness of figs and how nicely they pair with walnuts. I've left the broccoli raw here, as a tribute to the deli where I was first introduced to this dish. (I'm talking to you, Nature's Oasis in Durango, Colorado.) The raw broccoli adds a pleasant crunch and fresh flavor as well as the extra bonus of enzymes, with none of the nutrient levels reduced by cooking. This colorful salad is a lovely side but can also be a main dish if served over a whole grain such as couscous or quinoa.

1 cup stemmed and quartered dried figs (about 8 figs)

¾ cup thinly sliced red onion

½ cup chopped or halved raw walnuts

2 tablespoons extra-virgin olive oil

2 tablespoons pure maple syrup

1 tablespoon Dijon mustard

½ teaspoon sea salt

2 cups chopped broccoli florets

1 medium carrot, grated

1. In a medium bowl, combine the figs, onion, walnuts, olive oil, maple syrup, mustard, and salt. Stir well.

2. Add the broccoli and carrot and toss to thoroughly combine with the dressing. If possible, allow the salad to marinate in the fridge for several hours, or overnight, to lightly tenderize the broccoli and marinate the flavors. Serve cold or at room temperature. Store in an airtight container in the refrigerator for up to 4 days.

Per Serving: Calories: 240; Total Fat: 10g; Saturated Fat: 1g; Protein: 4g; Carbs: 38g; Fiber: 6g; Sodium: 309mg; Iron: 2mg

ZESTY CHICKPEA SALAD

GLUTEN-FREE, NUT-FREE, SOY-FREE   **SERVES 4**   **PREP TIME: 10 MINUTES**

This flavor-packed, high-fiber, protein-rich salad celebrates the magic of all things lemon. To me, lemons are the essential mascot of Mediterranean food—bright, fresh, and satisfying. Plus, fresh lemon with its alkalinizing properties is incredibly good for you. Serve this yummy salad alone, or alongside some Moroccan Couscous (page 103) or Potato Soup with Za'atar and Marcona Almonds (page 91) for a flavorful, satisfying meal.

2 (15-ounce) cans chickpeas *or* 3 cups cooked chickpeas, rinsed and drained

2 tablespoons extra-virgin olive oil

2 teaspoons grated lemon zest

¼ cup freshly squeezed lemon juice

2 teaspoons Dijon mustard

2 tablespoons minced fresh flat-leaf parsley

4 garlic cloves, minced or pressed

½ teaspoon sea salt

½ teaspoon freshly ground black pepper

2 cups chopped baby spinach

1. In a large bowl, toss together the chickpeas, olive oil, lemon zest and juice, mustard, parsley, garlic, salt, and pepper.

2. Divide the spinach among serving plates and top with the chickpea salad. Serve cold or at room temperature. Store the chickpea salad in an airtight container in the refrigerator for up to 5 days.

Love Your Leftovers: Have some fresh lemon juice leftover? That's a great problem to have. In fact, I strive to keep fresh lemon (and lime) juice on hand at all times and store it in a glass container in the fridge. It's so much better than bottled juice, and it keeps for about a week. For longer storage, you can pour the juice into ice cube trays and freeze individually. Then, pop out a "juice cube" and thaw anytime you need a zesty citrus kick.

Per Serving: Calories: 165; Total Fat: 8g; Saturated Fat: 1g; Protein: 6g; Carbs: 20g; Fiber: 1g; Sodium: 444mg; Iron: 5mg

CATALONIAN KALE SALAD

GLUTEN-FREE, NUT-FREE, SOY-FREE   **SERVES 4 TO 6**   **PREP TIME: 10 MINUTES**

This luscious salad is a staple in our home. It's easy to make, incredibly nutrient dense, and absolutely delicious. Even my picky daughter requests it, which says a lot. Plus, it's chock-full of enzymes thanks to the fact that it's almost completely raw. If you've ever had a raw kale salad, chances are it wasn't so great. Far too often, the leaves are tough and it's underflavored. In this recipe, I present to you the three components of a perfect kale salad: texture, massage, and acidity. Start with a finely textured kale (by removing the stems and chopping it into fine pieces), massage it well with the marinade, and use an acid component to break down the kale leaves (in this case, we're using lemon juice). Enjoy this deliciousness alongside some Happy Hummus (page 23) and Za'atar Crisps (page 64) for a light meal.

12 cups loosely packed stemmed and finely sliced kale

¼ cup freshly squeezed lemon juice

2 tablespoons extra-virgin olive oil

2 tablespoons agave nectar

8 garlic cloves, minced or pressed

½ cup raisins

16 Kalamata olives, pitted and chopped

½ teaspoon sea salt

1. In a large bowl, combine the kale, lemon juice, olive oil, and agave. Using your hands, toss well to combine and then work the liquids into the kale. Knead the marinade firmly into the kale for about 1 minute so that it becomes soft and tenderized, as well as a darker shade of green. Put a little muscle into it—your hard work will pay off.

2. Add the garlic, raisins, olives, and salt. With a large spoon, stir well. Serve cold or at room temperature. Store in an airtight container in the refrigerator for up to 5 days.

Love Your Leftovers: Hate the idea of throwing away those fat little kale stems? Me, too. They're great tossed into smoothies (if you've got a high-speed blender) or made into green juices.

Per Serving: Calories: 276; Total Fat: 9g; Saturated Fat: 1g; Protein: 7g; Carbs: 47g; Fiber: 5g; Sodium: 481mg; Iron: 4mg

FALAFEL SALAD

GLUTEN-FREE, NUT-FREE, SOY-FREE   **SERVES 6**   **PREP TIME: 15 MINUTES / COOK TIME: 45 MINUTES**

What on earth could be more satisfying than a well-designed falafel salad? You've got everything here, folks—the crunch of freshly made falafel, a rainbow of nutrient-dense vegetables, and a healthy dose of creamy, delicious tahini dressing. Yum. I like to serve this salad with Za'atar Crisps (page 64) or Spanakopita (page 41) for a complete meal. For an extra fun kick, top each salad with a sprinkle of za'atar.

½ orange bell pepper

½ yellow bell pepper

10 cups chopped romaine lettuce

1 cup halved cherry or grape tomatoes

1 medium cucumber, chopped or sliced

½ small red onion, thinly sliced

1 recipe Falafel (page 44), freshly made

1 recipe Easy Tahini-Herb Dressing (page 26)

1. Preheat the oven to 400°F.

2. Place the bell peppers halves cut-side down on a rimmed baking sheet. Roast for 30 minutes, or until lightly browned. Cut into strips.

3. Divide the lettuce among serving plates and top with the roasted peppers, tomatoes, cucumber, and onion. Add the hot falafel balls and drizzle with the tahini dressing. Serve immediately.

Super Easy: If you'd rather not spend time roasting the peppers, you can replace them with jarred roasted red peppers or additional tomatoes and cucumbers. Alternatively, add some finely chopped red cabbage or yellow tomatoes as another way to bring a variety of textures, colors, and nutrients to your meal.

Per Serving: Calories: 521; Total Fat: 27g; Saturated Fat: 4g; Protein: 16g; Carbs: 53g; Fiber: 13g; Sodium: 283mg; Iron: 14mg

ANYTIME VEGETABLE-LENTIL SOUP

GLUTEN-FREE, NUT-FREE, SOY-FREE   **SERVES 6**   **PREP TIME: 5 MINUTES / COOK TIME: 1 HOUR**

I usually have all of these ingredients on hand at all times, hence the title. This soup is just the thing to warm you up on a cold night or rainy day. Lentils are a wonderful source of fiber, protein, and other great nutrients. I suggest green or brown, but feel free to use any variety here. Serve with some Olive Bruschetta (page 43) or Mediterranean Avocado Toast (page 58) for a hearty meal.

2 tablespoons extra-virgin olive oil

2 medium carrots, thinly sliced

1 onion, chopped

7 cups water

1 russet potato, peeled and chopped

1 cup dried green or brown lentils

1 (14.5-ounce) can diced tomatoes

5 garlic cloves, minced or pressed

10 Kalamata olives, pitted and chopped

2 teaspoons dried oregano

3 bay leaves (optional)

1½ teaspoons sea salt

½ teaspoon freshly ground black pepper

1. In a large pot, heat the olive oil over medium-high heat. Add the carrots and onion and sauté for 5 minutes, or until the veggies begin to soften.

2. Add the water, potato, lentils, tomatoes and their juices, garlic, olives, oregano, and bay leaves (if using). Bring to a boil over high heat.

3. Reduce the heat to low and simmer, partially covered, until the lentils are soft, about 1 hour. Give the pot a brief stir a few times during this hour.

4. Once the lentils are tender, remove and discard the bay leaves (if using), stir in the salt and pepper, and serve. Store leftovers in an airtight container in the refrigerator for up to 1 week.

Tasty Tip: If you want to take this soup to the next level, jazz it up with any (or all) of the following additions: Garnish with fresh basil, sprinkle with za'atar, or spoon a dollop of Macadamia-Rosemary Cheese (page 27) on top.

Per Serving: Calories: 307; Total Fat: 6g; Saturated Fat: 1g; Protein: 14g; Carbs: 52g; Fiber: 13g; Sodium: 563mg; Iron: 4mg

CREAMY WHITE BEAN AND GREENS SOUP

GLUTEN-FREE, SOY-FREE   SERVES 5   PREP TIME: 10 MINUTES / COOK TIME: 5 MINUTES

This luscious soup is comfort in a bowl. It's creamy and rich, but with zero cholesterol or unhealthy ingredients. You can vary the greens with what's looking the most gorgeous at your local market. Whether it's kale, collards, or chard that's saying "pick me," be sure to remove any large stems, as they can be a bit tough—although if spinach is what's catching your eye, there's no need to de-stem as it's a very "soft" green. Enjoy with a piece of whole-grain bread or Za'atar Crisps (page 64) for ultimate happiness.

3 (15-ounce) cans great northern beans or cannellini beans or 4½ cups cooked beans, rinsed and drained

2½ to 3 cups unsweetened plain cashew milk or any nondairy milk, divided

¼ cup raw unsalted cashew pieces

1½ cups loosely packed finely chopped greens (such as spinach, kale, collards, or chard)

6 tablespoons freshly squeezed lemon juice

2 tablespoons extra-virgin olive oil

5 garlic cloves, minced or pressed

1 tablespoon dried dill

1½ teaspoons sea salt

1 teaspoon freshly ground black pepper

1. In a blender, process the beans, 2½ cups of milk, and cashews until velvety smooth.

2. Transfer the mixture to a soup pot and stir in the greens, lemon juice, olive oil, garlic, dill, salt, and pepper. If you prefer a thinner soup, add up to ½ cup more milk now.

3. Cook over medium-low heat, stirring often, until the greens are wilted, about 5 minutes. Serve hot or warm. Store leftovers in an airtight container in the refrigerator for up to 5 days.

Technique Tip: If you don't have a high-speed blender, soak the cashews for a few hours beforehand, then drain before using (so that they're soft enough to blend smooth).

Per Serving: Calories: 226; Total Fat: 10g; Saturated Fat: 1g; Protein: 10g; Carbs: 23g; Fiber: 11g; Sodium: 459mg; Iron: 3mg

ROASTED RED PEPPER SOUP

GLUTEN-FREE, SOY-FREE   **SERVES 4**   **PREP TIME: 5 MINUTES / COOK TIME: 30 MINUTES**

This humble soup is a delicious powerhouse of omega-rich cashews and antioxidant-rich garlic and basil. Although it's good on its own, it's also delicious topped with a dollop of Macadamia-Rosemary Cheese (page 27) and/or some homemade croutons. You can also simply garnish it with some thinly sliced basil and roughly chopped Marcona almonds. This makes a very satisfying meal alongside a salad such as The Vegan Greek (page 79) or Fattoush Salad (page 78).

Olive oil cooking spray

1 red bell pepper, halved and seeded

1 pound tomatoes, roughly chopped

½ cup raw unsalted cashew pieces

⅓ cup fresh basil

2 garlic cloves, peeled

1 teaspoon sea salt

¼ teaspoon freshly ground black pepper

¾ to 1 cup water

1. Preheat the oven to 400°F. Lightly spray a rimmed baking sheet with cooking spray.

2. Place the pepper halves, cut-side down, on the prepared sheet. Roast for 30 minutes, or until they're soft and have brown patches.

3. In a high-speed blender, combine the roasted peppers, tomatoes, cashews, basil, garlic, salt, pepper, and ¾ cup of water and process until very smooth. If you prefer a thinner soup, add up to ¼ cup additional water.

4. Transfer the soup to a small pot and warm over medium heat. Serve immediately.

Technique Tip: If you don't have a high-speed blender, soak the cashews in water for a few hours beforehand, then drain before using (so that they're soft enough to blend smooth).

Simple Swap: If you're having trouble finding decent fresh tomatoes, you can substitute canned ones. To do so, I'd recommend measuring out the liquid as well, so that you can use it in place of the water (or at least part of it). Start with a 14-ounce can of whole peeled tomatoes and add more if needed.

Per Serving: Calories: 120; Total Fat: 7g; Saturated Fat: 1g; Protein: 4g; Carbs: 12g; Fiber: 2g; Sodium: 467mg; Iron: 1mg

LEMONY LENTIL SOUP

GLUTEN-FREE, NUT-FREE, SOY-FREE   **SERVES 6**   **PREP TIME: 5 MINUTES / COOK TIME: 40 MINUTES**

This vibrant soup is absolutely bursting with lemony deliciousness. Lemon zest is a superb source of both flavor and vitamin C, and the juice does wonders to alkalinize the body. This is a great soup to help stave off a cold, impress guests, or satisfy every lemony desire you've ever had. Enjoy a bowl of this with Za'atar Crisps (page 64) and Broccoli, Walnut, and Fig Salad (page 83) for a blissfully nourishing meal.

3 tablespoons extra-virgin olive oil

1 onion, minced

6 cups water

1 cup plus 2 tablespoons dried red lentils

Grated zest of 1 lemon (about 2 teaspoons)

⅓ cup freshly squeezed lemon juice

½ cup plain unsweetened oat milk or other nondairy milk

4 garlic cloves, minced or pressed

2 teaspoons sea salt

Freshly ground black pepper

1. In a large pot, heat the oil over medium-high heat. Add the onion and sauté for about 10 minutes, stirring often, until soft and lightly browned.

2. Add the water, lentils, and lemon zest and stir well. Bring to a boil, then reduce the heat to low and simmer the soup, stirring occasionally, until the lentils are very soft, about 30 minutes.

3. Remove the pot from the heat and stir in the lemon juice, oat milk, garlic, salt, and pepper. Stir well and cover with a lid. Let sit for a few minutes, to "cook" the garlic into the soup. Stir again and serve. Store leftovers in an airtight container in the refrigerator for up to 1 week.

Tasty Tip: For extra nutrients and flavor, stir about 2 cups finely chopped, stemmed kale into the soup with the garlic, lemon juice, and final additions. You can also add 2 tablespoons of fresh dill or thyme to the soup while it has about 10 minutes left, for an additional flavor boost.

Per Serving: Calories: 194; Total Fat: 8g; Saturated Fat: 1g; Protein: 9g; Carbs: 22g; Fiber: 11g; Sodium: 560mg; Iron: 3mg

POTATO SOUP WITH ZA'ATAR AND MARCONA ALMONDS

SOY-FREE   **SERVES 4**   **PREP TIME: 5 MINUTES / COOK TIME: 35 MINUTES**

Creamy, dreamy potato soup topped with the unique tang of za'atar and crunchy, irresistible Marcona almonds? Yes, please. This hearty, satisfying soup is full of potassium, vitamin C, and fiber. Plus, it's ready in under 40 minutes. If you decide to make a double batch so you can enjoy lots of leftovers, be sure to reserve the za'atar and Marcona almonds until you're ready to serve so they retain their punch and crunch.

3 cups peeled, chopped potato

2 cups water

3 tablespoons extra-virgin olive oil, divided

¾ cup minced onion

2 tablespoons whole-wheat pastry flour, brown rice flour, or gluten-free all-purpose flour

1 cup plain unsweetened nondairy milk, divided

4 garlic cloves, minced or pressed

1 tablespoon freshly squeezed lemon juice

1 teaspoon sea salt

½ teaspoon freshly ground black pepper

3 to 4 tablespoons za'atar

¼ cup roughly chopped Marcona almonds

1. In a large pot, combine the potatoes and water and bring to a boil over medium-high heat. Cook for 20 minutes, or until soft. Remove from the heat and mash the potatoes into the water to form a creamy base, using a fork or potato masher. Set aside.

2. While the potatoes are cooking, in a medium skillet, heat 1 tablespoon of oil over medium heat and sauté the onion, stirring often, for about 10 minutes, or until golden brown and soft. Sprinkle in the flour and stir well. Add 2 tablespoons of milk and stir again. Slowly add ½ cup of milk, stirring or whisking well, until thoroughly combined.

3. Add this mixture to the potatoes and stir. Add the remaining 6 tablespoons of milk, 2 tablespoons of olive oil, garlic, lemon juice, salt, and pepper. Stir well and cook over low heat for 3 to 5 minutes to marry the flavors. Remove the soup from the heat and serve each bowl topped with the za'atar and almonds.

Simple Swap: If you can't find za'atar, you can substitute 3 tablespoons minced fresh dill. And you can replace the Marcona almonds with regular slivered almonds that have been lightly toasted in a dry pan.

Per Serving: Calories: 281; Total Fat: 15g; Saturated Fat: 2g; Protein: 6g; Carbs: 32g; Fiber: 5g; Sodium: 471mg; Iron: 2mg

VIBRANT BUTTERNUT AND BROCCOLI SOUP

GLUTEN-FREE, OIL-FREE, SOY-FREE　　　**SERVES 8**　　　**PREP TIME: 10 MINUTES / COOK TIME: 25 MINUTES**

This soup is like a vegan Greek version of broccoli cheese soup, and it's one of my all-time favorites for so many reasons. It's ever so pretty to look at, chock-full of beta-carotene and antioxidants, and comes together in about half an hour. This recipe makes a large batch, but I love it that way! I find it's wonderful to have plenty on hand throughout the week. It keeps well and makes a satisfying and nourishing meal in a hurry, especially with some bread and salad.

3 cups chopped red or gold potatoes

3 cups peeled, chopped butternut squash

1 onion, chopped

4 cups water

½ cup raw unsalted cashew pieces

¼ cup chopped roasted red pepper

¼ cup freshly squeezed lemon juice

¼ cup nutritional yeast

1½ teaspoons sea salt

¼ teaspoon ground turmeric

5 garlic cloves, minced or pressed

4 cups chopped broccoli florets

1. In a large pot, combine the potatoes, squash, onion, and water. If you don't have a high-speed blender, add the cashews at this point as well. Bring to a boil over high heat. Reduce the heat to low and simmer for 20 minutes, or until the potatoes and squash are tender. Remove the pot from the heat.

2. In a blender, combine the red pepper, lemon juice, nutritional yeast, salt, turmeric, garlic, and cashews (if you're using a high-speed blender). Add about 1 cup of the liquid from the soup pot to the blender and purée until velvety smooth. Add the remaining contents of the soup pot to the blender and process until very smooth. If your blender is small, you'll need to do this in batches.

3. Return everything to the soup pot and add the broccoli. Cook over medium-low heat, stirring often, for about 3 minutes until the broccoli is crisp-tender and bright green. Serve hot or warm.

Ingredient Tip: Butternut squash is fabulous to eat but a little intimidating to peel. Here's what I recommend for peeling one of these babies: Grab a sturdy vegetable peeler, get a firm grip, and peel in downward strokes. Alternatively, you can use a sharp chef's knife—just be careful. Or, if you'd rather just make it ultra-easy, pick up some frozen organic butternut squash chunks and call it good.

Per Serving: Calories: 152; Total Fat: 5g; Saturated Fat: 1g; Protein: 8g; Carbs: 23g; Fiber: 6g; Sodium: 390mg; Iron: 2mg

SUMMERY TOMATO-BASIL SOUP

GLUTEN-FREE, SOY-FREE   **SERVES 4**   **PREP TIME: 10 MINUTES / COOK TIME: 10 MINUTES**

Tomatoes, basil, and summer—how unbeatable is that combination? There's nothing like picking an abundance of fresh tomatoes from the garden and finding creative ways to use them all up. That's my version of heaven! Tomatoes contain high levels of the antioxidant lycopene, which has been linked to health benefits such as reduced risk of heart disease and cancer. Plus, you've got the immune-boosting properties of garlic and anti-inflammatory herbs such as basil to really give this soup a healthy kick. Sheer happiness!

2 tablespoons extra-virgin olive oil

¾ cup chopped onion

½ cup chopped celery

1 (15-ounce) can tomato sauce

3 ripe tomatoes, roughly chopped

½ cup water, plus more as needed

¼ cup raw unsalted cashew pieces

¼ cup packed fresh basil leaves

3 garlic cloves, peeled

1½ teaspoons dried oregano

1 teaspoon dried thyme

1 teaspoon sea salt

¼ teaspoon freshly ground black pepper

1. In a medium pot, heat the olive oil over medium-high heat and sauté the onion and celery in the oil, stirring often, for 3 to 5 minutes, until the onion just begins to brown.

2. Transfer the onion-celery mixture to a blender. Add the tomato sauce, tomatoes, water, cashews, basil, garlic, oregano, thyme, salt, and pepper. Blend until very smooth. If desired, add a little additional water to thin (the amount required will vary depending on how watery your tomatoes are).

3. Pour the contents of the blender back into the soup pot and bring to a boil over medium-high heat. Reduce the heat to low and simmer the soup for about 5 minutes to marry the flavors. If the soup is too thick, add a small amount of water until the desired consistency is reached. Serve warm or hot.

Technique Tip: If you don't have a high-speed blender, soak the cashews in water for a few hours beforehand, then drain them before using (so that they're soft enough to blend smooth).

Love Your Leftovers: Do you need to use up the rest of that fresh basil you got for this soup? There are lots of ways to do that—in pasta, on garlic toast, and as a tasty garnish for dips. You can also add it to fresh lemonade for a delicious twist, or freeze in ice cube trays (with water) to preserve for later use.

Per Serving: Calories: 165; Total Fat: 11g; Saturated Fat: 2g; Protein: 4g; Carbs: 16g; Fiber: 4g; Sodium: 532mg; Iron: 2mg

PROVENÇAL ZUCCHINI SOUP

NUT-FREE, SOY-FREE   SERVES 4   PREP TIME: 5 MINUTES / COOK TIME: 30 MINUTES

When summertime hits and you have too much zucchini (as if that's possible), this soup is perfection on a hot afternoon. It's a pretty green color, and has the fun twist of a piece of garlic bread on top for some crunch. Zucchini is a great source of fiber, helps lower blood sugar levels, and is high in antioxidants. If you're gluten free, you can easily substitute a gluten-free bread for the baguette, or simply omit it and serve with your favorite gluten-free crackers.

2 tablespoons extra-virgin olive oil, divided

1 leek (white and pale green parts only), rinsed well and roughly chopped

4 garlic cloves, minced or pressed, divided

3 zucchini, cut into 1-inch pieces (about 6 cups)

4 cups vegetable broth or vegan "chicken" broth

2 teaspoons herbes de Provence

1 bay leaf

8 thin slices baguette

Sea salt

Freshly ground black pepper

1. In a large soup pot, heat 1 tablespoon of olive oil over medium-low heat. Add the leek and sauté until softened, 5 to 7 minutes. Add half of the garlic and cook, stirring constantly, for 1 minute.

2. Add the zucchini, broth, herbes de Provence, and bay leaf. Bring the soup to a boil over medium-high heat. Reduce the heat to low and simmer for about 20 minutes.

3. While the soup is cooking, preheat the oven or toaster oven to 400°F.

4. In a small bowl, combine the remaining 1 tablespoon of olive oil with the remaining garlic. Brush the toasted baguette slices with the mixture, sprinkle the tops lightly with salt, and place them directly on the oven rack. Bake for 5 to 10 minutes until golden brown.

5. When the soup is finished cooking, remove and discard the bay leaf. Transfer the soup to a blender or use an immersion blender to purée it until smooth. Season with salt and pepper to taste. Ladle into soup bowls and float two garlic toasts on top in each bowl.

Technique Tip: If you're using a countertop blender to purée hot liquids, be sure to remove the center cap from the lid and hold a clean dish towel over the hole to allow steam to escape.

Ingredient Tip: Leeks can be dirty little babies that collect a lot of debris in between their layers. To clean them, cut off the tough green leaves. Leaving the root intact, cut the leek in half lengthwise. Under running water, hold apart the layers to rinse away the dirt trapped inside.

Per Serving: Calories: 232; Total Fat: 9g; Saturated Fat: 2g; Protein: 11g; Carbs: 28g; Fiber: 3g; Sodium: 389mg; Iron: 3mg

LEMONY ORZO SOUP

NUT-FREE　　　**SERVES 4 TO 6**　　　**PREP TIME: 10 MINUTES / COOK TIME: 25 MINUTES**

This summery soup is light and refreshing, yet filling, thanks to chunks of protein-packed tofu and chewy orzo. It's also high in iron and beta-carotene, thanks to the spinach and carrots, and cholesterol free, thanks to the fact that it's plant based. Orzo wants you to know that it's actually pasta, even though it looks like rice. Don't mind the identity crisis, though—orzo is deliciously worth any confusion.

2 tablespoons extra-virgin olive oil

1 onion, chopped

2 carrots, peeled and chopped

2 celery stalks, thinly sliced

6 cups vegetable broth or vegetarian "chicken" broth

2 bay leaves

1 cup orzo

8 ounces extra-firm tofu, cut into ½-inch cubes

4 garlic cloves, minced or pressed

2 cups baby spinach

2 lemons, 1 halved and 1 thinly sliced

Sea salt

Freshly ground black pepper

1. In a large soup pot, heat the olive oil over medium heat. Add the onion, carrots, and celery and sauté until softened, 5 to 7 minutes.

2. Add the broth and bay leaves and bring the soup to a boil. Add the orzo, tofu, and garlic. Reduce the heat to low and simmer for 12 to 15 minutes until the orzo is tender. Stir in the spinach and squeeze the juice from the halved lemon into the soup. Stir over low heat for 30 to 60 seconds, until the spinach is wilted. Remove and discard the bay leaves and season with salt and pepper. Ladle the soup into bowls and top each bowl with a slice of lemon.

Per Serving: Calories: 208; Total Fat: 8g; Saturated Fat: 1g; Protein: 8g; Carbs: 29g; Fiber: 3g; Sodium: 170mg; Iron: 2mg

ROASTED PINE NUT ORZO, P. 109

MAINS

CHICKPEA MEDLEY

GLUTEN-FREE, NUT-FREE, OIL-FREE, SOY-FREE   **SERVES 4**   **PREP TIME: 5 MINUTES**

This recipe is easy as can be, and perfect for when you just want something tasty and healthy in a pinch—it's not mind-blowing, but it's incredibly functional, and has saved me on numerous occasions! Coconut aminos aren't very Mediterranean, you may be muttering under your breath, but I use them here because they lend a lovely, rich flavor and make for an easy dressing. This salad dressing is my go-to dressing when I travel, because it's so easy to whip up, even in a hotel room, and it satisfies my taste buds and hunger. You'll be glad you gave it a shot!

2 tablespoons tahini

2 tablespoons coconut aminos

1 (15-ounce) can chickpeas *or* 1½ cups cooked chickpeas, rinsed and drained

1 cup finely chopped lightly packed spinach

1 carrot, peeled and grated

1. In a medium bowl, whisk together the tahini and coconut aminos.

2. Add the chickpeas, spinach, and carrot to the bowl. Stir well and serve at room temperature. Store leftovers in an airtight container in the refrigerator for up to 1 week.

Simple Swap: Coconut aminos are almost like a sweeter, mellower version of soy sauce. However, if you want to use regular soy sauce or tamari, just use 1½ tablespoons and add a dash of maple syrup or agave nectar to balance out the saltiness.

Per Serving: Calories: 161; Total Fat: 6g; Saturated Fat: 1g; Protein: 7g; Carbs: 22g; Fiber: 6g; Sodium: 38mg; Iron: 3mg

MOROCCAN COUSCOUS

OIL-FREE, NUT-FREE, SOY-FREE   SERVES 4   PREP TIME: 10 MINUTES / COOK TIME: 5 MINUTES

Ah, couscous! Fun to say *and* fun to eat. (Some actually say the name is derived from the sound it makes as it cooks!) Couscous pasta is made from durum wheat and is a staple throughout North Africa. Gorgeous Moroccan spices like cumin, cinnamon, and paprika lend sweet, savory, and earthy undertones to every bite. For an extra treat, drizzle with some Luscious Moroccan Sauce (page 29) and top with crunchy pistachio nuts.

1 cup couscous

1½ cups water

1½ teaspoons grated orange or lemon zest

¾ cup freshly squeezed orange juice

4 or 5 garlic cloves, minced or pressed

2 tablespoons raisins

2 tablespoons pure maple syrup or agave nectar

2¼ teaspoons ground cumin

2¼ teaspoons ground cinnamon

¼ teaspoon paprika

2½ tablespoons minced fresh mint

2 teaspoons freshly squeezed lemon juice

½ teaspoon sea salt

1. In a medium pot, combine the couscous and water. Add the orange zest and juice, garlic, raisins, maple syrup, cumin, cinnamon, and paprika and stir. Bring the mixture to a boil over medium-high heat.

2. Remove the couscous from the heat and stir well. Cover with a tight-fitting lid and set aside until all of the liquids are absorbed and the couscous is tender and fluffy. Gently stir in the mint, lemon juice, and salt. Serve warm or cold. Store leftovers in an airtight container in the refrigerator for up to 5 days.

Ingredient Tip: Depending on what type of couscous you use, you may need to add a bit more liquid. Generally, whole-grain couscous tends to need more liquid, so if you find yours is a bit dry, add more juice or water as needed.

Simple Swap: For a gluten-free option, you can substitute quinoa or rice for the couscous. Also, use the lemon zest instead of orange zest if you prefer a tangier end result.

Per Serving: Calories: 242; Total Fat: 1g; Saturated Fat: 0g; Protein: 7g; Carbs: 53g; Fiber: 3g; Sodium: 244mg; Iron: 2mg

ALETHEA'S LEMONY ASPARAGUS PASTA

NUT-FREE, SOY-FREE   **SERVES 6**   **PREP TIME: 10 MINUTES / COOK TIME: 20 MINUTES**

My daughter's name, Alethea, means "truth" in Greek. So, believe her when she tells you that this dish is one you absolutely *must* try. She's actually a bit obsessed with it—she even requested it for her birthday the past two years. We prefer it with a neutral-flavored oil, but if you want an olive-flavored kick, feel free to substitute extra-virgin olive oil. Either way, it's scrumptious—and perfect for everything from weekday eats to birthday parties!

1 pound spaghetti, linguini, or angel hair pasta

2 crusty bread slices

½ cup plus 1 tablespoon avocado oil, divided

3 cups chopped asparagus (1½-inch pieces)

½ cup vegan "chicken" broth or vegetable broth, divided

6 tablespoons freshly squeezed lemon juice

8 garlic cloves, minced or pressed

3 tablespoons finely chopped fresh curly parsley

1 tablespoon grated lemon zest

1½ teaspoons sea salt

1. Bring a large pot of water to a boil over high heat and cook the pasta until al dente according to the instructions on the package.

2. Meanwhile, in a medium skillet, crumble the bread into coarse crumbs. Add 1 tablespoon of oil to the pan and stir well to combine over medium heat. Cook for about 5 minutes, stirring often, until the crumbs are golden brown. Remove from the skillet and set aside.

3. Add the chopped asparagus and ¼ cup of broth in the skillet and cook over medium-high heat until the asparagus is bright green and crisp-tender, about 5 minutes. Transfer the asparagus to a very large bowl.

4. Add the remaining ½ cup of oil, remaining ¼ cup of broth, lemon juice, garlic, parsley, zest, and salt to the asparagus bowl and stir well.

5. When the noodles are done, drain well, and add them to the bowl. Gently toss with the asparagus mixture. Just before serving, stir in the toasted bread crumbs. Store leftovers in an airtight container in the refrigerator for up 2 days.

Ingredient Tip: For the pasta, I recommend Jovial brown rice capellini as it's made from nutritious whole grains yet tastes very light. The bread is also your choice, whether you want sprouted, whole-grain, artisanal bread, or gluten free.

Per Serving: Calories: 526; Total Fat: 23g; Saturated Fat: 3g; Protein: 13g; Carbs: 68g; Fiber: 10g; Sodium: 1422mg; Iron: 6mg

MOROCCAN TEMPEH

GLUTEN-FREE, NUT-FREE　　　**SERVES 4**　　　**PREP TIME: 20 MINUTES / COOK TIME: 20 MINUTES**

This dish is full of nutrients and absolutely luscious, from the crunch of the tempeh to the sweet and savory sauce. Tempeh is a high-fiber whole food that's a great source of plant-based protein. Plus, it's fermented, so it's good for the immune system and digestion. It's delicious when prepared correctly, so if you haven't liked tempeh in the past, give this recipe a shot! You can serve this as is, or over couscous or quinoa.

1 pound plain tempeh

1 cup water

¼ cup tamari, shoyu, or soy sauce

1½ cups gluten-free all-purpose flour

½ cup cornmeal

¼ cup sesame seeds

1 teaspoon paprika

1 teaspoon sea salt

1 teaspoon freshly ground black pepper

1 cup plain unsweetened nondairy milk

½ cup sunflower oil

1 recipe Luscious Moroccan Sauce (page 29)

1. Gently slice the tempeh into 8 rectangular cutlets that are approximately 2½ by 4 inches in size and ½ inch thick, or half their original thickness. Place them in a single layer in a large skillet. Evenly pour the water and tamari on top. Turn the cutlets over to coat both sides with the liquid. Cover and cook over medium heat for 5 minutes. Flip the cutlets, cover, and cook for another 5 minutes, or until all of the liquid has been absorbed. Transfer the tempeh to a plate and wipe out the skillet. Set aside.

2. In a shallow bowl, mix the flour, cornmeal, sesame seeds, paprika, salt, and pepper. Pour the milk into another shallow bowl.

3. In the now-empty skillet, heat the oil over medium-high heat. While it is heating, dip a tempeh cutlet in the milk, and then in the flour coating. Then dip the tempeh in the milk again, then in the flour coating a second time to form an even, thick layer of coating on all sides. Repeat with all the tempeh cutlets.

4. Working in batches, pan-fry the cutlets for about 2 minutes on each side until golden brown. Remove and drain on paper towels.

5. Place each tempeh cutlet on a plate, drizzle with the sauce, and serve immediately.

Tasty Tip: To take this dish up another notch, serve over Moroccan Couscous (page 103) and garnish with any (or all) of the following: pomegranate seeds, minced fresh cilantro, toasted almond slivers, or crushed pistachios.

Simple Swap: Extra-firm tofu makes a perfectly suitable stand-in for the tempeh. If you do opt for tofu, you can skip adding water to the pan, and simply drizzle the tofu slices with the tamari before coating them.

Per Serving: Calories: 968; Total Fat: 54g; Saturated Fat: 8g; Protein: 30g; Carbs: 98g; Fiber: 8g; Sodium: 2175mg; Iron: 7mg

PASTA WITH LEMON AND ARTICHOKES

NUT-FREE, SOY-FREE   **SERVES 4**   **PREP TIME: 10 MINUTES / COOK TIME: 15 MINUTES**

This simple dish comes together in about 20 minutes, and it's so yummy and satisfying (especially if you're artichoke-obsessed like me). Those glorious little vegetables are not only delicious, they're also packed with good-for-you benefits. Artichokes are high in fiber and are known for reducing inflammation, improving digestion, and lowering unhealthy (LDL) cholesterol. Plus, they magically seem to make any dish they're added to extra special!

16 ounces linguine or angel hair pasta

¼ cup extra-virgin olive oil

8 garlic cloves, finely minced or pressed

2 (15-ounce) jars water-packed artichoke hearts, drained and quartered

2 tablespoons freshly squeezed lemon juice

¼ cup thinly sliced fresh basil

1 teaspoon sea salt

Freshly ground black pepper

1. Bring a large pot of water to a boil over high heat and cook the pasta until al dente according to the directions on the package.

2. While the pasta is cooking, heat the oil in a skillet over medium heat and cook the garlic, stirring often, for 1 to 2 minutes until it just begins to brown. Toss the garlic with the artichokes in a large bowl.

3. When the pasta is done, drain it and add it to the artichoke mixture, then add the lemon juice, basil, salt, and pepper. Gently stir and serve.

Tasty Tip: For extra deliciousness, substitute 3 cups Lemony Grilled Artichokes (page 46) for the jars of artichokes. You can also grate a little lemon zest over the top for an extra kick or top the pasta with ¼ cup Kalamata olives. Or, if you really want to take this dish to the next level, do all three!

Simple Swap: To make this recipe gluten free, I recommend Jovial brown rice capellini as it's made from nutritious whole grains yet still tastes very light.

Per Serving: Calories: 423; Total Fat: 14g; Saturated Fat: 2g; Protein: 15g; Carbs: 64g; Fiber: 18g; Sodium: 650mg; Iron: 6mg

ROASTED PINE NUT ORZO

SOY-FREE　　　**SERVES 4**　　　**PREP TIME: 10 MINUTES / COOK TIME: 15 MINUTES**

Commonly served in Greek cuisine, orzo looks like rice but it's actually a type of pasta. It has a uniquely chewy and rather luscious consistency when cooked to perfection. Don't skip toasting the pine nuts here—it brings out their buttery, rich flavor, which does wonders in this recipe. You can feel confident serving this delectable entrée for weekday meals, or to impress special guests!

16 ounces orzo

1 cup diced roasted red peppers

¼ cup pitted, chopped Kalamata olives

4 garlic cloves, minced or pressed

3 tablespoons olive oil

1½ tablespoons freshly squeezed lemon juice

2 teaspoons balsamic vinegar

1 teaspoon sea salt

¼ cup pine nuts

¼ cup packed thinly sliced or torn fresh basil

1. Bring a large pot of water to a boil over medium-high heat and add the orzo. Cook, stirring often, for 10 minutes, or until the orzo has a chewy and firm texture. Drain well.

2. While the orzo is cooking, in a large bowl, combine the peppers, olives, garlic, olive oil, lemon juice, vinegar, and salt. Stir well.

3. In a dry skillet, toast the pine nuts over medium-low heat until aromatic and lightly browned, shaking the pan often so that they cook evenly. Watch them closely, as this process will take only about 2 minutes. When lightly browned, immediately remove the pine nuts from the pan and set aside.

4. Stir the orzo into the pepper-olive mixture and mix well. Serve topped with the pine nuts and basil.

Ingredient Tip: Orzo will double in size when cooked. However, if it's kept in the liquid longer, it will grow bigger until all of the cooking liquid has been absorbed. Be sure to drain it immediately upon reaching the desired texture and add it to the sauce mixture within a minute or so, to avoid clumping.

Per Serving: Calories: 424; Total Fat: 22g; Saturated Fat: 3g; Protein: 9g; Carbs: 49g; Fiber: 3g; Sodium: 813mg; Iron: 3mg

GREEK FLATBREADS

NUT-FREE, SOY-FREE   SERVES 4   PREP TIME: 15 MINUTES / COOK TIME: 10 MINUTES

There was a Greek restaurant I used to visit in my hometown of South Bend, Indiana, that made a version of these flatbreads, which is when I first fell in love with the concept. Crisp, warm pita bread slathered with creamy hummus and topped with classic Greek toppings is a heavenly combination, I tell you. Serve with Quinoa Tabbouleh (page 80) or Vibrant Butternut and Broccoli Soup (page 92) and a few Delicious Dolmas (page 34) for a satisfying meal.

4 Pita Bread (page 65) rounds or store-bought pita rounds

1 recipe Happy Hummus (page 23)

2 cups baby spinach leaves

1 cup sliced grape tomatoes

½ cup pitted, halved Kalamata olives

½ cup thinly sliced red onion

⅓ cup thinly sliced fresh basil

¼ cup sliced Greek peperoncini (optional)

3 tablespoons extra-virgin olive oil (optional)

1. Preheat the oven to 350°F.

2. Place the pita rounds directly on the oven rack and bake for 5 to 10 minutes until lightly browned and crisp.

3. Place a pita on each plate. Spread the hummus evenly over each. Evenly distribute the spinach, tomatoes, olives, onion, basil, and peperoncini (if using) on top. Drizzle with olive oil (if using), then cut into quarters and serve immediately.

Simple Swap: You can use whole-grain or gluten-free tortillas instead of the pita rounds if you'd like.

Per Serving: Calories: 645; Total Fat: 32g; Saturated Fat: 4g; Protein: 23g; Carbs: 75g; Fiber: 15g; Sodium: 862mg; Iron: 7mg

MEDITERRANEAN MACRO PLATE

GLUTEN-FREE, NUT-FREE   **SERVES 6**   **PREP TIME: 15 MINUTES / COOK TIME: 10 MINUTES**

Sometimes I just want to eat something that's super light yet still satisfying. This "macro plate" offers just that. It's clean and healthy but also tasty and filling. It's also bread free, which makes it especially light. One thing that makes this extra tasty is the herbes de Provence, a traditional blend of aromatic herbs like oregano, sage, and lavender that grow in the hills of southern France during the summer.

6 cups cauliflower florets

8 ounces firm or extra-firm tofu

Olive oil cooking spray

1 tablespoon herbes de Provence

Sea salt

1 recipe Ful Medames (page 31)

1 recipe Happy Hummus (page 23)

6 cups sliced cucumber

1. Pour an inch or two of water into a large pot and insert a steamer rack. Bring the water to a boil, add the cauliflower, cover, and cook over medium heat until tender, about 10 minutes.

2. While the cauliflower is cooking, cut the tofu into 1-inch cubes. Heat a large skillet over medium-high heat. Spray with cooking spray and lay the tofu in a single layer in the skillet. Sprinkle evenly with the herbes de Provence and salt. Cook for 4 minutes, or until the undersides are golden brown. Spray with cooking spray, flip, and cook for an additional 3 to 4 minutes until golden brown on the other side. Remove from the heat.

3. Divide the ful medames and hummus among 6 plates. Add a scoop of tofu and cauliflower to each plate and divide the cucumber for dipping into the hummus. Serve immediately.

Simple Swap: If you prefer, substitute broccoli, asparagus, Brussels sprouts, or another vegetable for the cauliflower. You can also swap out the Happy Hummus for Classic Baba Ghanoush (page 22), Tangy Cheese Dip (page 25), or Vibrant Beet Hummus (page 24). This recipe lends itself to lots of variations, so have fun mixing it up!

Per Serving: Calories: 559; Total Fat: 23g; Saturated Fat: 3g; Protein: 27g; Carbs: 67g; Fiber: 13g; Sodium: 469mg; Iron: 7mg

THE ATHENA PIZZA

SOY-FREE   SERVES 4   PREP TIME: 15 MINUTES / COOK TIME: 10 MINUTES

Athena is the Greek goddess of wisdom and skill. You're wise for adding this dish to your repertoire, because it's nutrient dense, ridiculously tasty, and easy to make. However, it doesn't take much skill. Things that may seem complicated (like making vegan cheese from scratch) are actually quite easy when you follow these simple instructions. Serve this yummy pizza alongside Zesty Chickpea Salad (page 84) or some steamed vegetables for a supremely satisfying, nourishing meal.

4 Pita Bread (page 65) rounds or store-bought pita bread

6 cups lightly packed stemmed and thinly sliced kale

2 tablespoons freshly squeezed lemon juice

1 tablespoon extra-virgin olive oil

4 garlic cloves, finely minced or pressed

¼ teaspoon sea salt

1 recipe Macadamia-Rosemary Cheese (page 27)

1 cup halved grape or cherry tomatoes

½ cup pitted, chopped Kalamata olives

1. Preheat the oven to 400°F.

2. Arrange the pita bread rounds in a single layer on two large rimmed baking sheets. Bake for 5 to 10 minutes until golden brown and crisp. Remove and set aside.

3. In a large bowl, mix the kale, lemon juice, and olive oil. Using your hands, work the lemon and oil into the kale, squeezing firmly, so that the kale becomes soft and tenderized, as well as a darker shade of green. Stir in the garlic and salt.

4. Assemble the pizzas by spreading each pita with a generous coating of macadamia cheese and topping evenly with the kale salad, tomatoes, and olives. Cut each pizza into quarters and serve immediately.

Ingredient Tip: People often wonder what kind of kale to use when eating it raw. Honestly, you can use any kind, but I tend to gravitate toward green or red curly kale because of their mild flavor, which leaves plenty of room for the flavors of the marinade to come through.

Simple Swap: You can use whole-grain or gluten-free tortillas instead of the pita rounds if you prefer.

Per Serving: Calories: 616; Total Fat: 39g; Saturated Fat: 6g; Protein: 16g; Carbs: 57g; Fiber: 10g; Sodium: 740mg; Iron: 6mg

MUJADARA

GLUTEN-FREE, NUT-FREE, SOY-FREE   SERVES 4   PREP TIME: 5 MINUTES / COOK TIME: 45 MINUTES

Mujadara's origins are in Iraq, and today it's a popular dish across the Middle East and Eastern Mediterranean. It's also one of my favorites. The heartiness of the rice and lentils paired with luscious caramelized onions is an irresistible combination. This dish is packed with protein, iron, and fiber and is healthier than typical versions, as it's made with whole-grain rice. Serve this with Falafel Salad (page 86), Delicious Dolmas (page 34), and some Happy Hummus (page 23) for a healthy feast.

¾ cup dried brown lentils

¼ cup long-grain brown rice

3 cups vegetarian "chicken" broth or vegetable broth

5 garlic cloves, minced or pressed

2 tablespoons extra-virgin olive oil, divided

4 cups thinly sliced onion

Sea salt

1 teaspoon balsamic vinegar

1. In a large pot, combine the lentils, rice, broth, and garlic and bring to a boil over high heat. Reduce the heat to low, partially cover the pot, and simmer for 45 minutes, or until the lentils and rice are tender and the water is absorbed.

2. While the lentils and rice are cooking, heat a large skillet over medium-low heat. Add 1 tablespoon of oil and the onion. Cook, stirring often, for 40 minutes, or until the onions are very well browned and caramelized. If the pan becomes too dry at any point, add water as needed and stir. Once done, remove from the heat and season with salt.

3. When the lentils and rice are done, stir in the vinegar and remaining 1 tablespoon of oil and season with salt. Serve the lentil-rice mixture topped with the caramelized onions.

Ingredient Tip: Vegetarian "chicken" broth offers a rich, balanced flavor that works beautifully here. You can find it on the shelves of most supermarkets and health food stores in the soup section. However, if you have trouble finding a "chicken" broth, you can use a vegetable broth instead.

Per Serving: Calories: 281; Total Fat: 8g; Saturated Fat: 1g; Protein: 12g; Carbs: 43g; Fiber: 7g; Sodium: 68mg; Iron: 3mg

BRIAM

GLUTEN-FREE, NUT-FREE, SOY-FREE **SERVES 4** **PREP TIME: 10 MINUTES / COOK TIME: 1 HOUR**

This simple, rustic dish of saucy roasted vegetables is a Greek staple that's flavored with tomatoes, garlic, and herbs. My version is even lighter and simpler than the traditional version, as I use a fraction of the oil and slice the potatoes thinly to reduce cooking time. This goes nicely with Zesty Chickpea Salad (page 84) and Delicious Dolmas (page 34), although it's also delightful served simply with a little bread on the side for scooping up any saucy remains.

Olive oil cooking spray

2 medium zucchini, cut into ½-inch-thick rounds

2 gold potatoes, thinly sliced

4 tomatoes, sliced

1¾ cups tomato sauce

10 garlic cloves, cut into large chunks

1½ tablespoons olive oil

4 teaspoons dried basil

2 teaspoons dried oregano

1 teaspoon sea salt

1. Preheat the oven to 400°F. Spray a large baking dish lightly with cooking spray.

2. In a large bowl, combine the zucchini, potatoes, tomatoes, tomato sauce, garlic, olive oil, basil, oregano, and salt and stir well. Pour the vegetable mixture into the prepared dish.

3. Bake for 30 minutes, stir well, and bake for another 30 minutes, or until the potatoes are tender. Stir again and serve.

Tasty Tip: For an extra treat, toast ¼ cup pine nuts over low heat in a dry pan, shaking often, for 2 minutes or until lightly browned. Immediately remove from the heat and sprinkle on top of the finished briam. You can also garnish with fresh basil for a pop of extra flavor.

Simple Swap: For a fun twist, substitute eggplant and/or red or yellow bell peppers for some or all of the zucchini.

Per Serving: Calories: 338; Total Fat: 20g; Saturated Fat: 3g; Protein: 7g; Carbs: 39g; Fiber: 9g; Sodium: 835mg; Iron: 4mg

ZUCCHINI BOATS WITH COUSCOUS STUFFING

NUT-FREE, SOY-FREE   **SERVES 4**   PREP TIME: 10 MINUTES / COOK TIME: 40 MINUTES

It doesn't like to brag, but Israeli couscous is bigger than traditional couscous and has a delightfully chewy texture and fun appearance. However, if you can't find Israeli couscous, the regular kind will work just fine. For a balanced meal, serve this with some Delicious Dolmas (page 34) and Classic Baba Ghanoush (page 22) on the side.

1 tablespoon olive oil, plus more for greasing pan

2 large zucchini

1¼ cups vegetarian "chicken" broth or vegetable broth

1 cup Israeli couscous

3 shallots, minced

1 cup canned or fresh diced tomatoes

1 tablespoon capers

2 tablespoons za'atar

2 cups chopped arugula

Sea salt

Freshly ground black pepper

1. Preheat the oven to 400°F. Lightly grease a large baking dish with oil.

2. Cut each zucchini in half lengthwise. Use a spoon to scoop out the seeds and enough interior flesh to make a deep trough. If possible, leave the flesh intact where the stem end was so the stuffing won't fall out. Arrange the zucchini, cut-side up, in the prepared dish.

3. In a medium saucepan, bring the broth to a simmer. Add the couscous, cover the pan, and cook for 8 minutes, or until just tender. Remove from the heat and let sit for 2 to 3 minutes, then drain excess liquid if needed.

Continued on next page

4. Meanwhile, in a large skillet, heat the oil over medium heat. Add the shallots and sauté for 3 to 4 minutes, stirring frequently. Add the tomatoes and their juices, capers, and za'atar. Cook, stirring frequently, for about 3 minutes. Add the cooked couscous and arugula and sauté for 2 to 4 minutes until the arugula is wilted and the mixture is saucy, but not watery. Remove the filling from the heat and season with salt and pepper.

5. Spoon the couscous filling into the zucchini boats and bake for 25 minutes, or until the zucchini is tender. Remove and serve warm or hot.

Ingredient Tip: If using regular couscous, prepare it by bringing 1½ cups water to a boil. Stir in the couscous, then remove the pan from the heat, cover, and let it sit for 5 minutes, or until the couscous has absorbed all of the water and is tender. Proceed with the recipe as instructed.

Per Serving: Calories: 235; Total Fat: 4g; Saturated Fat: 1g; Protein: 8g; Carbs: 42g; Fiber: 5g; Sodium: 149mg; Iron: 1mg

PASTA WITH CREAMY TOMATO SAUCE

OIL-FREE, SOY-FREE   **SERVES 4**   **PREP TIME: 10 MINUTES / COOK TIME: 10 MINUTES**

I've been making this pasta sauce for almost thirty years! However, instead of my '90s version with oil and soy milk, I've substituted whole-food cashews for the creaminess factor. It's delicious, very easy to make, and extremely nutrient dense. It makes the perfect Mediterranean-inspired meal, especially when served with Catalonian Kale Salad (page 85) or Cucumbers in Tahini-Dill Sauce (page 37).

---

16 ounces linguine

2 cups chopped onion

1 cup chopped carrot

½ cup dry white wine

½ cup raw unsalted cashew pieces

¼ to ½ cup water

2 (14.5-ounce) cans diced tomatoes

4 garlic cloves, peeled

24 large basil leaves, 12 left whole and 12 cut into thin ribbons

1 teaspoon sea salt

¼ teaspoon freshly ground black pepper

1. Bring a large pot of water to a boil over high heat and cook the pasta until al dente according to the directions on the package. Drain.

2. Meanwhile, in a large skillet, combine the onion, carrot, and wine. (If you're not using a high-speed blender, add the cashews now as well.) Sauté the vegetables over medium heat for 5 minutes, stirring often. As you go, add the water, as needed, to prevent sticking.

3. Add the tomatoes and their juices. Cook, stirring often, for another 5 minutes.

Continued on next page

4.   Transfer the mixture to a high-speed blender. Add the garlic, whole basil leaves, cashews, salt, and pepper. Blend until very smooth.

5.   Serve generous portions of the sauce over the pasta and top with the fresh basil ribbons.

Technique Tip: Whenever you use a countertop blender to purée hot liquids, be sure to remove the center cap from the lid and hold a clean dishtowel over the hole to allow steam to escape.

Tasty Tip: For extra flavor, add a dollop of Macadamia-Rosemary Cheese (page 27) to the top of your pasta before sprinkling it with basil. It will be even prettier and richer tasting.

Simple Swap: To make this gluten free, I recommend Jovial brown rice capellini as it's made from nutritious whole grains yet still tastes very light.

Per Serving: Calories: 532; Total Fat: 11g; Saturated Fat: 2g; Protein: 17g; Carbs: 85g; Fiber: 8g; Sodium: 503mg; Iron: 4mg

SPICY EGGPLANT POLENTA

GLUTEN-FREE, SOY-FREE   **SERVES 4**   **PREP TIME: 10 MINUTES / COOK TIME: 30 MINUTES**

There's just nothing like succulent eggplant to give you that "meaty" satisfaction, especially when it's soaking in a delicious, enticing sauce such as this one. Although polenta traditionally takes a very long time to cook, I've found you can cheat the system successfully with this quick-cook method, which involves bringing it to a boil first, then whisking often. If you want an even easier, quicker substitution, you can also use premade polenta (in tubes). Simply slice and pan-fry it and top with the eggplant mixture.

For the polenta

1 cup cornmeal

3¼ cups water

2 tablespoons olive oil

3 tablespoons nutritional yeast

½ to ¾ teaspoon sea salt

For the eggplant

2 pounds eggplant, peeled and cut into small cubes (about 12 cups)

3 tablespoons olive oil

2 to 4 cups water, divided

1 cup tomato sauce

5 garlic cloves, minced or pressed

4 teaspoons harissa paste

¼ cup pine nuts

1 teaspoon sea salt

2 tablespoons thinly sliced fresh basil

To make the polenta

1. In a medium-large pot, combine the cornmeal and water and cook over medium heat, whisking constantly, until it begins to thicken. Once it begins to thicken a bit, turn the heat down to the lowest setting possible. Continue to cook, whisking very often, for 10 minutes, or until thick. If you desire a slightly thinner consistency, whisk in a bit more water.

2. Remove the polenta from the heat and whisk in the oil, nutritional yeast, and salt. Set aside.

Continued on next page

To make the eggplant

1. In a large skillet or wok, combine the eggplant, olive oil, and 2 cups of water. Cook over medium-high heat, stirring often, for 5 minutes.

2. Add the tomato sauce, garlic, and harissa and reduce the heat to medium-low. Continue to cook, stirring often, for 10 minutes, or until the eggplant is very soft. You will need to add up to 2 more cups of water during this process, depending on your variety of eggplant. I typically use all 4 cups in order to reach the desired sauciness level. What you're aiming for is a thick (but still saucy and wet) tomato sauce.

3. While the tomato sauce is cooking, in a dry skillet, toast the pine nuts over low heat, shaking often, for 2 minutes, or until lightly browned and aromatic.

4. Once the eggplant is tender, stir in the salt. Ladle the polenta onto plates and top with the eggplant mixture. Finish with a sprinkle of toasted pine nuts and fresh basil.

Simple Swap: If you don't have harissa, just omit it, or add a dash of cayenne or Aleppo pepper instead.

Per Serving: Calories: 406; Total Fat: 29g; Saturated Fat: 3g; Protein: 12g; Carbs: 32g; Fiber: 13g; Sodium: 1319mg; Iron: 3mg

GREEK TOSTADAS

GLUTEN-FREE, NUT-FREE, SOY-FREE   **SERVES 6**   **PREP TIME: 15 MINUTES / COOK TIME: 10 MINUTES**

You may be suspicious of merging Greek and Mexican food, but there's something so satisfying about a crunchy tostada shell topped with creamy hummus, rich avocado, and a rainbow of glorious vegetables. This delicious entrée also packs immense heart-healthy nutrition: iron- and protein-rich chickpeas, whole-grain corn, potassium-rich avocados, immune-boosting garlic and lemon, and energizing, cleansing kale. I recommend serving these tostadas with some Summery Tomato-Basil Soup (page 94) on the side for the perfect meal.

Olive oil cooking spray

6 (6-inch) corn tortillas

7 cups stemmed and finely chopped lacinato or curly kale

2 tablespoons freshly squeezed lemon juice

1 tablespoon extra-virgin olive oil

2 garlic cloves, minced or pressed

¼ teaspoon sea salt

1 recipe Happy Hummus (page 23)

2 avocados, peeled, pitted, and chopped

¾ cup finely chopped purple cabbage

2 tomatoes, chopped

2 limes or lemons, quartered (optional)

1. Preheat the oven to 400°F. Spray a rimmed baking sheet with cooking spray.

2. Arrange the tortillas in a single layer on the prepared sheet. Spray the tops generously with oil and bake for 5 to 10 minutes until lightly browned and crisp. Set aside.

3. In a large bowl, combine the kale, lemon juice, and olive oil. Using your hands, work the lemon and oil into the kale, squeezing firmly, so that the kale becomes soft and tenderized, as well as a darker shade of green. Stir in the garlic and salt.

4. To assemble, top the baked tortillas with a generous layer of hummus. Top evenly with the massaged kale, avocado chunks, cabbage, and tomatoes. If desired, serve with lime or lemon wedges for squeezing over the top.

Simple Swap: If you prefer flour tortillas to corn, feel free to substitute them here. In a pinch, you can also use baby spinach instead of the kale salad. Just be sure to serve your tostadas with the lemon wedges (and a dash of sea salt) if you do, since you'll be omitting those flavors from the kale salad.

Per Serving: Calories: 474; Total Fat: 28g; Saturated Fat: 4g; Protein: 13g; Carbs: 48g; Fiber: 13g; Sodium: 307mg; Iron: 5mg

RASPBERRY CHEESECAKE SQUARES, P. 132

DESSERTS

CHOCOLATE HUMMUS

GLUTEN-FREE, NUT-FREE, OIL-FREE, SOY-FREE   **SERVES 6**   **PREP TIME: 10 MINUTES**

Chocolate hummus? Is that even legal? Trust me, I hear you. I resisted the chocolate hummus trend until I created this recipe. But this velvety, rich chocolate treat made me a believer, and I know it will knock your socks off, too! There are so many reasons to love it. First of all, it's healthy. It doesn't have added oils, refined sweeteners, or flours, unlike most desserts. Plus, it's got the added iron, protein, and fiber of chickpeas, as well as the antioxidants of cacao. And finally, it makes you feel like you're eating a fluffy, chocolate cloud (or spoonfuls of frosting, at the very least) without a single unhealthy ingredient.

1 (15-ounce) can chickpeas *or* 1½ cups cooked chickpeas, rinsed and drained

¼ cup cacao powder

6 tablespoons pure maple syrup or agave nectar

¼ cup unsweetened vanilla or plain nondairy milk, plus more as needed

1 tablespoon vanilla extract

½ teaspoon sea salt

1. In a blender or food processor, combine the chickpeas, cacao powder, maple syrup, nondairy milk, vanilla, and salt. Blend until as smooth as possible. You will likely have enough liquid to blend, but if not, add another tablespoon or two of nondairy milk (I've found certain brands of chickpeas require more).

2. Once velvety smooth, serve immediately, or store in an airtight container in the fridge for up to a week.

Serving Tip: This chocolate hummus is great just plain, and that's how I usually eat it to be perfectly honest. Hello, spoon! However, it's also delicious as a dip for strawberries or bananas. Or you can serve it topped with some chocolate chips and a dollop of peanut butter for extra pizzazz.

Per Serving: Calories: 133; Total Fat: 3g; Saturated Fat: 2g; Protein: 5g; Carbs: 28g; Fiber: 4g; Sodium: 239mg; Iron: 3mg

PISTACHIO BAKLAVA

SOY-FREE **MAKES 15 BARS** **PREP TIME: 20 MINUTES / COOK TIME: 35 MINUTES**

This traditional Greek dessert is so scrumptious and impressive you won't believe how easy it is to make. It's perfect for special occasions, potlucks, or anytime you want to impress your guests with a knockout dish. If you've never worked with phyllo before, don't worry—it's pretty forgiving. If you break or tear it, no biggie. Just lay it down in the pan as if nothing happened. No one will ever know.

½ cup agave nectar

¼ cup plus 1 tablespoon organic sugar, divided

2 whole cinnamon sticks

3 whole cardamom pods

3 whole cloves

1 teaspoon vanilla extract

½ teaspoon freshly squeezed lemon juice

¼ teaspoon sea salt, divided

½ cup water

½ cup shelled pistachios

1 teaspoon ground cinnamon

8 ounces phyllo dough, thawed overnight in the refrigerator

6 to 8 tablespoons nondairy margarine, melted, or sunflower oil

1. Preheat the oven to 350°F.

2. In a small saucepan, combine the agave, ¼ cup of sugar, cinnamon sticks, cardamom pods, cloves, vanilla, lemon juice, and $\frac{1}{8}$ teaspoon of salt. Add the water and bring the mixture to a boil over medium heat. Reduce the heat to low and simmer gently for 15 minutes, stirring occasionally. Set aside. Once cooled, remove and discard the cinnamon sticks, cardamom pods, and cloves.

3. In a food processor, chop the pistachios until coarsely ground. Mix the crushed nuts with the cinnamon, remaining 1 tablespoon of sugar, and remaining $\frac{1}{8}$ teaspoon of salt. Stir well and set aside.

Continued on next page

4. Divide the phyllo dough in half. Set half aside, covered with a lightly damp towel. Using a pastry brush, coat the bottom and sides of a 9-by-9-inch baking pan with melted margarine.

5. Place one sheet of phyllo (from the uncovered stack) on the bottom of the pan and brush it lightly with margarine. If your phyllo doesn't fit exactly in the pan, simply cut it or overlap it a bit. Continue layering one piece of phyllo at a time, brushing each piece lightly with margarine until you've used up the first half of the dough. Top the phyllo evenly with the nut mixture.

6. Uncover the second portion of the phyllo and repeat the layering process on top of the nut mixture, brushing each layer with margarine as you go.

7. When you've used all the phyllo, use a sharp knife to cut diagonal lines 1½ inches apart across the whole pan. If it helps, hold on to the top layer of phyllo with your other hand as you make parallel cuts all the way through to the bottom of the pan. Next, cut vertical lines, also 1½ inches apart, down the length of the pan, to create diamond-shaped pieces.

8. Pour half of the reserved sauce evenly over the top of the phyllo. Bake for 20 to 30 minutes, until nicely golden brown.

9. Remove the pan from the oven. Pour the remaining sauce evenly over the top of the baklava. This may seem like a lot of sauce, but the longer the baklava sits, the less saucy and sweet it becomes. Allow the baklava to cool slightly and enjoy. Store in an airtight container in the refrigerator for up to 1 week.

Ingredient Tip: Not feeling the pistachios—or don't have them on hand? You can replace them with walnuts, almonds, or pecans. It's nutty how delicious this baklava is with any of them.

Per Serving: Calories: 159; Total Fat: 8g; Saturated Fat: 1g; Protein: 2g; Carbs: 21g; Fiber: 1g; Sodium: 186mg; Iron: 1mg

MARCONA-LEMON BARS

SOY-FREE **SERVES 12** **PREP TIME: 10 MINUTES, PLUS 30 MINUTES CHILLING / COOK TIME: 50 MINUTES**

If you're in the mood for a flavor party—and you're a lemon lover—this is the dessert for you. It's a symphony of tastes and textures, and perfect for impressing guests and for any special occasions. Here's to the good life!

For the crust

1½ cups whole-wheat pastry flour or gluten-free all-purpose flour

¼ cup confectioners' sugar

1 teaspoon dried rosemary

½ cup sunflower or avocado oil, plus more for greasing

½ cup chopped roasted Marcona almonds

For the filling

1½ cups granulated sugar

¾ cup freshly squeezed lemon juice

¾ cup unsweetened applesauce

4 tablespoons packed grated lemon zest, divided

¼ teaspoon sea salt

2 teaspoons baking powder

2 tablespoons arrowroot powder or cornstarch

1 teaspoon dried rosemary

To make the crust

1. In a medium bowl, stir together the flour, confectioners' sugar, rosemary, and sunflower oil until well combined. Cover the bowl with plastic and refrigerate for 30 minutes or more.

2. Preheat the oven to 350°F. Lightly grease an 8-by-11½-inch pan with sunflower oil.

3. Put the almonds in a zip-top plastic bag, seal it, and lay it on the counter. Smash the bag with a can or jar, or run a rolling pin over the top, until the nuts are crushed. They shouldn't be obliterated, just lightly crushed into pea-size pieces. Set aside.

4. Press the dough firmly into the baking dish and bake for 5 to 10 minutes.

5. Remove the pan from the oven and sprinkle the almonds evenly over the top of the crust. Set aside while you make the filling.

Continued on next page

To make the filling

1. In a small bowl, mix the granulated sugar, lemon juice, applesauce, 3 tablespoons of lemon zest, and salt. Add the baking powder and arrowroot and stir well.

2. Pour the filling evenly over the crust, on top of the almonds. Bake for 30 to 40 minutes until the crust is nicely browned (it's better to undercook than overcook—even if the filling doesn't look totally done, remove it if the crust is brown and much of the filling looks firm). The filling will firm up more upon cooling, especially if you can refrigerate it for several hours or overnight.

3. After the lemon bars have cooled slightly, sprinkle the remaining 1 tablespoon of lemon zest and rosemary over the top, cut into squares, and serve. Store leftovers in an airtight container in the refrigerator for 4 to 5 days.

Per Serving: Calories: 267; Total Fat: 11g; Saturated Fat: 2g; Protein: 3g; Carbs: 43g; Fiber: 2g; Sodium: 43mg; Iron: 0mg

VEGAN PASTELI

GLUTEN-FREE, OIL-FREE, SOY-FREE   **SERVES 10 TO 12**   **PREP TIME: 5 MINUTES / COOK TIME: 20 MINUTES**

Pasteli is a simple sesame seed–based Greek dessert that's typically made with honey and white sugar. This vegan version is made without refined sugars but is still as addictively delicious. It's kind of a cross between an energy snack and a dessert, but it will definitely satisfy your craving for something sweet at the end of a meal. You can feel extra great about this tasty dessert as it's high in fiber, omega-3s, calcium, and iron, and offers the additional health benefits of lemon zest.

1 cup sesame seeds

⅓ cup whole almonds

½ cup pure maple syrup

¼ cup coconut sugar

¼ teaspoon sea salt

1 teaspoon grated lemon zest

1. Preheat the oven to 400°F. Line an 8-inch pie pan or baking pan with parchment paper.

2. In a large nonstick or stainless steel skillet, toast the sesame seeds over medium-low heat, shaking the pan often, for 5 to 7 minutes. Remove the pan from the heat as soon as they become lightly golden brown and aromatic. Be very careful, as they can get overly browned in a flash if you're not paying close attention. Remove the seeds from the pan quickly to avoid additional cooking and set aside to cool.

3. Put the almonds in a zip-top plastic bag, seal it, and lay it on the counter. Smash the bag with a can or jar, or run a rolling pin over the top, until the nuts are crushed. They shouldn't be obliterated, just lightly crushed into pea-size pieces. Set aside.

4. In a medium pot, combine the maple syrup, coconut sugar, and salt. Bring the mixture to a boil over medium-high heat. Reduce the heat to low and simmer, whisking often, for about 5 minutes. Remove the pot from the heat and stir in the lemon zest. Add the sesame seeds and almonds and stir well with a spoon.

Continued on next page

5. Pour the mixture into the prepared pan and spread it out, flattening with a spatula. Press it down into the pan firmly and evenly. Bake the pastelli for 5 to 10 minutes until the sesame seeds are just slightly more browned than before. Remove from the oven and let cool for 10 minutes or so. Once the pasteli is slightly cool, but still soft enough to cut, take a sharp knife and cut into individual pieces. If you wait too long and your mixture is too hard to cut, no worries. Just grab it out of the pan (parchment paper and all) and break it into 10 to 12 pieces.

6. Store in an airtight container at room temperature for up to 1 week (if you have lots of willpower, that is).

Per Serving: Calories: 160; Total Fat: 9g; Saturated Fat: 1g; Protein: 3g; Carbs: 20g; Fiber: 2g; Sodium: 50mg; Iron: 2mg

BERRY COMPOTE WITH LEMONY CREAM

GLUTEN-FREE, SOY-FREE   **SERVES 6**   **PREP TIME: 5 MINUTES**

This dessert is so simple but so delightful. There's something just heavenly about vibrant, antioxidant-rich berries, topped with a rich, creamy lemon sauce. It absolutely sends me. I recommend using a variety of berries for maximum visual (and flavor) impact. My favorite combination is equal parts strawberries, blueberries, and raspberries. This treat also doubles as a supremely satisfying breakfast when topped with a little granola.

1 cup raw unsalted cashew pieces

½ cup pure maple syrup

¼ cup water

2 teaspoons packed grated lemon zest

3 tablespoons freshly squeezed lemon juice

2 tablespoons sunflower or avocado oil

2 teaspoons vanilla extract

¼ teaspoon sea salt

9 cups fresh berries

In a high-speed blender, combine the cashews, maple syrup, water, lemon zest and juice, oil, vanilla, and salt and process until completely smooth and velvety. Remove and serve on top of the berries. Any leftover sauce will keep in an airtight container in the fridge for a week or more.

Technique Tip: If you're not using a high-speed blender, soak the cashews in enough water to cover them for several hours so that they're soft enough to blend smooth. Once soaked, drain off the water and blend with the other ingredients.

Per Serving: Calories: 315; Total Fat: 16g; Saturated Fat: 3g; Protein: 5g; Carbs: 42g; Fiber: 5g; Sodium: 88mg; Iron: 3mg

RASPBERRY CHEESECAKE SQUARES

GLUTEN-FREE, SOY-FREE   SERVES 9   PREP TIME: 15 MINUTES, PLUS 1 HOUR CHILLING

Although cheesecake isn't traditionally a Greek dessert, this one has all the components of a Mediterranean approach—it's plant based, nutrient dense, lemony, and a delicious celebration of life. Plus, the pistachio-date crust gives it a lovely Greek foundation that's simply irresistible. You may also notice that this is a completely uncooked dessert. That's no accident. I absolutely love a raw cheesecake, because it's so vibrant, nourishing, and fresh tasting. I hope you love this knee-buckling dessert as much as I do.

For the crust

1 cup shelled pistachios

½ cup packed pitted dates

⅛ teaspoon sea salt

For the filling

1½ cups raw unsalted cashews, soaked for several hours in water and drained (no need to soak if you're using a high-speed blender)

½ cup agave nectar

½ cup freshly squeezed lemon juice

¼ cup sunflower or avocado oil

4 teaspoons vanilla extract

½ teaspoon sea salt

⅛ teaspoon ground nutmeg

¾ cup fresh raspberries, for topping

To make the crust

In a food processor, blend the pistachios, dates, and salt until sticky and crumbly, but with a bit of texture remaining. If the mixture does not stick together, blend a bit longer or add a few more dates until it does. Press the dough firmly into the bottom of an 8-by-8-inch baking pan and place it in the freezer.

To make the filling

In a food processer or high-speed blender, blend the cashews, agave, lemon juice, oil, vanilla, salt, and nutmeg until velvety smooth. Pour onto the crust and smooth out the top. Top with the raspberries (open-sides down) and refrigerate for 1 to 2 hours, or until firm. Cut into squares and serve.

Tasty Tip: For extra raspberry love, you can artfully swirl a little fruit-sweetened raspberry jam into the cheesecake filling before topping with the fresh raspberries.

Per Serving: Calories: 349; Total Fat: 19g; Saturated Fat: 3g; Protein: 4g; Carbs: 45g; Fiber: 4g; Sodium: 112mg; Iron: 2mg

CHOCOLATEY PEANUT BUTTER AND BANANA BITES

GLUTEN-FREE, OIL-FREE, SOY-FREE   **SERVES 4**   **PREP TIME: 5 MINUTES**

This is one of my go-to desserts for so many reasons. First of all, it's absurdly delicious. I may or may not have been swearing under my breath (due to unreasonable yumminess) when I created this recipe. Secondly, it literally takes under 5 minutes to make. And finally, it's healthy, low in fat, and full of fiber, potassium, and antioxidants. It's truly a feel-good treat that will also feel oh-so-satisfying, which is at the heart of our friend, the Mediterranean lifestyle!

¼ cup peanut butter powder

¼ cup cacao powder

¼ cup pure maple syrup

¼ cup unsweetened plain or vanilla almond milk or other nondairy milk

1 teaspoon vanilla extract

¼ teaspoon sea salt

4 firm bananas, cut into ½-inch-thick rounds

1. In a bowl, whisk together the peanut butter powder, cacao powder, maple syrup, almond milk, vanilla, and salt until lump free and smooth. Set aside.

2. Divide the bananas onto serving plates. Serve with the sauce either drizzled over the top of the bananas or on the side as a dip. If you have any sauce leftover, store it in an airtight container in the refrigerator for up to 1 week.

Ingredient Tip: Peanut butter powder is a low-fat, reduced-calorie swap for regular peanut butter. I enjoy it as a lighter way to get my peanut butter fix, and it works wonderfully in shakes, savory peanut sauces, and sweet desserts such as this one. If you prefer to go the regular peanut butter route, you can use smooth peanut butter in place of the powder, and thin the sauce with additional almond milk if needed.

Per Serving: Calories: 235; Total Fat: 5g; Saturated Fat: 3g; Protein: 7g; Carbs: 52g; Fiber: 10g; Sodium: 163mg; Iron: 2mg

STRAWBERRY CREAM AND MARCONA PARFAITS

GLUTEN-FREE   **SERVES 6**   **PREP TIME: 10 MINUTES**

Really good Mediterranean food doesn't rely on complexity to be fabulous. It's crave-worthy because of the wonderful flavors of often simple ingredients. This dessert is no exception. Even though it's quite simple (just nondairy cream, nuts, and fruit), it's totally satisfying and refreshing. You can, of course, vary the berries here, or even add sliced banana. For extra flair, serve in pretty wine glasses so you can see the layers. You might want to whip up a big batch of the strawberry cream and keep it on hand, as the rest of the dessert comes together in about a minute.

2 (12.3-ounce) packages firm silken tofu

½ cup agave nectar

1½ tablespoons vanilla extract

8 large whole fresh or frozen strawberries plus 2 cups sliced fresh or frozen strawberries, divided

¼ cup sunflower oil

¼ teaspoon sea salt

1 cup raspberries or additional strawberries

½ cup roughly chopped Marcona almonds

1. In a food processor or blender, process the tofu, agave, vanilla, 8 whole strawberries, sunflower oil, and salt until velvety smooth.

2. Divide 1 cup of sliced strawberries into 6 serving bowls or glasses and top with the raspberries and half the strawberry cream. Finish with the remaining sliced strawberries, more strawberry cream, and the Marcona almonds.

Per Serving: Calories: 413; Total Fat: 16g; Saturated Fat: 2g; Protein: 10g; Carbs: 54g; Fiber: 6g; Sodium: 120mg; Iron: 2mg

ROASTED PEARS WITH PISTACHIOS

GLUTEN-FREE, OIL-FREE, SOY-FREE   **SERVES 4**   **PREP TIME: 5 MINUTES / COOK TIME: 25 MINUTES**

This recipe is simple yet elegant, and a great way to top off a meal, especially if you want something sweet that still leaves you feeling light and supercharged. Pistachios and pomegranate give this recipe an Eastern Mediterranean flair. You can also feel great about your choice to *not* skip dessert with this dish, as pears are high in fiber and antioxidants, and pomegranates are bursting with flavonoids and antioxidants. If you've made a habit of keeping some Pomegranate-Balsamic Reduction (page 28) on hand, this dish will come together in no time.

4 pears

1 lemon, halved

1 recipe Pomegranate-Balsamic Reduction (page 28)

½ cup chopped pistachios

1. Preheat the oven to 375°F. Pour ¼ inch of water into a nonstick baking dish.

2. Cut the pears in half lengthwise. Use a paring knife to notch out the stringy core running to the seeds, and use a spoon to scoop out the seeds. Rub each half with the lemon to prevent browning, then place them cut-side up in the prepared baking dish. Bake for 25 minutes, or until the pears are tender.

3. Place 2 baked pear halves in each of 4 shallow bowls. Spoon the pomegranate syrup over the pears and sprinkle with the pistachios.

Per Serving: Calories: 283; Total Fat: 4g; Saturated Fat: 0g; Protein: 2g; Carbs: 60g; Fiber: 7g; Sodium: 48mg; Iron: 1mg

ZUCCHINI BOATS WITH COUSCOUS STUFFING, P. 115

DIRTY DOZEN AND CLEAN FIFTEEN™

A nonprofit environmental watchdog organization called Environmental Working Group (EWG) looks at data about pesticide residues supplied by the United States Department of Agriculture (USDA) and the Food and Drug Administration (FDA). Each year it compiles a list of the best and worst pesticide loads found in commercial crops. You can use these lists to decide which fruits and vegetables to buy organic to minimize your exposure to pesticides and which produce is considered safe enough to buy conventionally. This does not mean they are pesticide-free, though, so wash these fruits and vegetables thoroughly. The list is updated annually, and you can find it online at EWG.org/FoodNews.

Dirty Dozen™

1. strawberries
2. spinach
3. kale
4. nectarines
5. apples
6. grapes
7. peaches
8. cherries
9. pears
10. tomatoes
11. celery
12. potatoes

Additionally, nearly three-quarters of hot pepper samples contained pesticide residues.

Clean Fifteen™

1. avocados
2. sweet corn
3. pineapples
4. sweet peas (frozen)
5. onions
6. papayas
7. eggplants
8. asparagus
9. kiwis
10. cabbages
11. cauliflower
12. cantaloupes
13. broccoli
14. mushrooms
15. honeydew melons

MEASUREMENT CONVERSIONS

VOLUME EQUIVALENTS (LIQUID)

US STANDARD	US STANDARD (OUNCES)	METRIC (APPROXIMATE)
2 tablespoons	1 fl. oz.	30 mL
¼ cup	2 fl. oz.	60 mL
½ cup	4 fl. oz.	120 mL
1 cup	8 fl. oz.	240 mL
1½ cups	12 fl. oz.	355 mL
2 cups or 1 pint	16 fl. oz.	475 mL
4 cups or 1 quart	32 fl. oz.	1 L
1 gallon	128 fl. oz.	4 L

OVEN TEMPERATURES

FAHRENHEIT (F)	CELSIUS (C) (APPROXIMATE)
250°	120°
300°	150°
325°	165°
350°	180°
375°	190°
400°	200°
425°	220°
450°	230°

VOLUME EQUIVALENTS (DRY)

US STANDARD	METRIC (APPROXIMATE)
⅛ teaspoon	0.5 mL
¼ teaspoon	1 mL
½ teaspoon	2 mL
¾ teaspoon	4 mL
1 teaspoon	5 mL
1 tablespoon	15 mL
¼ cup	59 mL
⅓ cup	79 mL
½ cup	118 mL
⅔ cup	156 mL
¾ cup	177 mL
1 cup	235 mL
2 cups or 1 pint	475 mL
3 cups	700 mL
4 cups or 1 quart	1 L

WEIGHT EQUIVALENTS

US STANDARD	METRIC (APPROXIMATE)
½ ounce	15 g
1 ounce	30 g
2 ounces	60 g
4 ounces	115 g
8 ounces	225 g
12 ounces	340 g
16 ounces or 1 pound	455 g

RESOURCES

Books

- Barnard, Neal. *Dr. Neal Barnard's Program for Reversing Diabetes* (Rodale Books, 2018).

- Buettner, Dan. *The Blue Zones: 9 Lessons for Living Longer from the People Who've Lived the Longest*, second edition (National Geographic, 2012).

- Challis, Tess. *Radiant Health, Inner Wealth; The Two-Week Wellness Solution; Radiance 4 Life; 100 Vegan Entrées; Food Love* (all available at tesschallis.com).

- Challis, Tess. *The Essential Vegan Air Fryer Cookbook* (Rockridge Press, 2019).

- Hever, Julieanna. *The Vegiterranean Diet* (Da Capo Lifelong Books, 2014).

- Moran, Victoria. *The Love-Powered Diet: Eating for Freedom, Health and Joy* (Lantern Books, 2009).

- Ruiz, Don Miguel. *The Four Agreements: A Practical Guide to Personal Freedom* (Amber-Allen Publishing, 2011).

- Wood, Rebecca. *The New Whole Foods Encyclopedia* (Penguin Books, 2010).

Websites

- TessChallis.com: Recipes, "one degree" inspiration, recommended kitchen products, and more.

- PlantBasedMuscles.com: A great resource for plant-based exercise and fitness

- JulieandKittee.com: Excellent recipes and resources for a vegan and gluten-free lifestyle

- WorldofVegan.com: A wonderful resource for new and seasoned vegans

REFERENCES

Buettner, Dan. *The Blue Zones: 9 Lessons for Living Longer from the People Who've Lived the Longest,* second edition (Washington, DC: National Geographic, 2012).

CardioSmart American College of Cardiology. "Study Confirms the Heart-Health Benefits of a Mediterranean Diet." Accessed April 18, 2019. https://www.cardiosmart.org /News-and-Events/2018/07/Study-Confirms-the-Heart-Health-Benefits-of-a -Mediterranean-Diet.

Harvard T. H. Chan School of Public Health. "Diet Review: Mediterranean Diet." Accessed April 18, 2019. https://www.hsph.harvard.edu/nutritionsource/healthy-weight/diet -reviews/mediterranean-diet.

Hever, Julieanna. *The Vegiterranean Diet.* (Boston: Da Capo Lifelong Books, 2014).

Mangels, Reed. "Protein in the Vegan Diet." Accessed April 18, 2019. The Vegetarian Resource Group, www.vrg.org/nutrition/protein.php.

Mayo Clinic. "Mediterranean Diet: A Heart-Healthy Eating Plan." Accessed April 18, 2019. https://www.mayoclinic.org/healthy-lifestyle/nutrition-and-healthy-eating/in-depth /mediterranean-diet/art-20047801.

McDougall, John. "A Revelation: Your Health Is Not Determined by Heredity." https://www .drmcdougall.com/health/education/free-mcdougall-program/introduction/revelation/.

Messina, Virginia. "The Vegan Mediterranean Diet" *One Green Planet.* Accessed April 18, 2019. https://www.onegreenplanet.org/natural-health/vegan-health/the-vegan -mediterranean-diet.

Physicians Committee for Responsible Medicine. "A Vegan Diet Is Healthier Than Traditional Mediterranean Diet." Accessed April 18, 2019. https://www.pcrm.org/news/blog/vegan -diet-healthier-mediterranean-diet.

Poore, J., and T. Nemecek. "Reducing Food's Environmental Impacts Through Producers and Consumers." *Science* 360, no. 639201 (June 2018): 987–992. doi:10.1126/science.aaq0216.

The McDougall Newsletter. "Fish Is Not Health Food." http://www.nealhendrickson.com/mcdougall/030200pufishisnothealthfood.htm.

———. "Protein Overload." https://www.drmcdougall.com/misc/2004nl/040100puproteinoverload.htm.

U.S. News and World Report. "U.S. News Reveals Best Diets Rankings in 2019." Accessed April 18, 2019. https://www.usnews.com/info/blogs/press-room/articles/2019-01-02/us-news-reveals-best-diets-rankings-for-2019.

RECIPE INDEX

INDEX

ACKNOWLEDGMENTS

This book wouldn't be possible without the amazing team at Callisto Media. It's such a joy to work with a publisher that believes in doing things right and supports the vision and integrity of its authors. My editor, Rachel, was especially lovely, and invaluable to the process. Thank you all.

I am, of course, grateful to my daughter, Alethea, for being one heck of a recipe tester—that girl has such a refined palate! She also provided moral support on long days of writing and testing and was always there to offer kind words and encouragement. Oh, how I love that human! My wonderful partner, John, was also a lifesaver throughout this process. There were times I couldn't see much of his sweet face because I was so busy writing and testing, but he never failed to be understanding and supportive. He also provided excellent feedback by taste-testing some of the recipes in this book—a job he probably didn't hate.

And a world of gratitude goes out to my amazing recipe testers. Without them, these recipes wouldn't be what they are today. Linzey Seiber, Nicole Lueders, Michelle Wilson, Jan Nicolet, Kathleen Evey Walters, and Jan Cawthorne—I appreciate your valuable feedback so very much! And Leslie Finnegan Conn, Anastacia Norris, Kathy Bethune, and Kassidy Bennett, you put forth a huge extra effort toward the end of this book, which basically saved me. You're rock stars and I can't thank you enough.

And last but certainly not least, I am thankful for you. I appreciate the fact that you're reading this and holding my book in your hands. I wouldn't be able to do this fun cookbook-writing thing if it wasn't for that. So, thank you!

ABOUT THE AUTHOR

Tess Challis is a renowned "One Degree Transformation Specialist," a seven-time author, a coach, and a speaker who helps women create their own recipes for success—for food and for life. She's been featured in the *Huffington Post* and on the website MindBodyGreen.com as well as on television networks, including ABC, NBC, and CBS. Tess lives in Phoenix, Arizona, and deals with the heat by drinking a bit too much kombucha. Get inspiration, recipes, and more info at TessChallis.com.

NOTES

NOTES

NOTES

NOTES

NOTES

NOTES

NOTES

NOTES

NOTES

NOTES

NOTES